T0244124

Home Run King

Home Run King

THE REMARKABLE RECORD
OF HANK AARON

DAN SCHLOSSBERG

FOREWORD BY DUSTY BAKER
PREFACE BY KEVIN BARNES

SPORTS
PUBLISHING

Sports Publishing books may be purchased in bulk at special discounts for sales promotion, corporate gifts, fund-raising, or educational purposes. Special editions can also be created to specifications. For details, contact the Special Sales Department, Sports Publishing, 307 West 36th Street, 11th Floor, New York, NY 10018 or sportspubbooks@skyhorsepublishing.com.

Sports Publishing® is a registered trademark of Skyhorse Publishing, Inc.®, a Delaware corporation.

Visit our website at www.sportspubbooks.com.

10 9 8 7 6 5 4 3 2 1

Library of Congress Cataloging-in-Publication Data is available on file.

Jacket design by David Ter-Avanesyan
Jacket photograph: Getty Images

Print ISBN: 978-1-68358-484-1
Ebook ISBN: 978-1-68358-485-8

Printed in the United States of America

This book is dedicated to the memory of baseball friends no longer with us, including Bob Feller, Milo Hamilton, Ernie Harwell, Monte Irvin, Ed Lucas, Stan Musial, and Phil Niekro.

Their friendly faces may be gone, but their memories will live forever.

TABLE OF CONTENTS

ACKNOWLEDGMENTS

This book would not have been possible without Julie Ganz, now Julie Perry, a Mets fan with whom I also worked on a half-dozen other Sports Publishing projects. She didn't ask for an outline, a table of contents, or a sample chapter, but she knew I was an ardent fan of the Braves in general and Hank Aaron in particular.

I miss Julie, who has left her post at Skyhorse, parent company of Sports Publishing, to pursue a new role as a full-time mother and part-time freelancer. At least she named the latest addition to her growing family Daniel.

I am also indebted to my kind and gracious editor, Jason Katzman, who stepped into Julie's shoes without missing a beat.

Thanks also to my terrific literary agent Rob Wilson, who fine-tuned contract offers from Julie and other publishers before allowing me to put my signature on them. He couldn't crack the Yankee lineup when Don Mattingly anchored first base but he's hit many home runs for Team Schlossberg.

On the other hand, my long-time friend Kevin Barnes has hit home runs against Team Schlossberg. We haven't played stickball in years (though we should have an Old Timers Day before we get older than Julio Franco) but he still brags about hitting my tennis-ball knuckler a long, long way.

A New Jersey native who now lives in Atlanta, where his various assignments include doing the stats for visiting broadcast crews at Truist Park, Kevin was instrumental in laying the groundwork for my interviews with Billye Aaron, Hank's widow; Lary Aaron, his son; and Braves manager Brian Snitker, whose 45-year sojourn in the Atlanta system started when Hank Aaron offered him a job as a minor-league manager.

Much of the material in this book came from my own interviews with Aaron, whose career I covered in my first book, *Hammerin' Hank: The Henry Aaron Story*, and hundreds of articles before and after. I appreciate all the editors who opened the door, including those at my hometown paper and first employer, the Passaic (NJ) *Herald-News*.

It was at the *Herald-News* where I first met Jay Horwitz, also a college intern at the time but on his way to an illustrious career as media relations director (and later alumni relations director) of the Mets. Jay put me in touch with Davey Johnson, who managed the Mets and other clubs years after he teamed with Aaron and Darrell Evans to become the first trio of teammates to hit 40 home runs in the same season.

Even before I wound up as a college intern myself, I met Aaron for the first time when I was sports editor of *The Hilltop Star* at Passaic High School at age seventeen in 1965. My assignment was to interview Bobby Bragan, then the manager of the Milwaukee Braves, about sportsmanship. But I got to meet Aaron too and do the first of dozens of interviews with the humble hero.

A myriad of baseball friends also provided personal memories of Aaron.

None were better than Dusty Baker, whom I befriended as a Braves rookie, even writing a magazine article entitled "The Next Hank Aaron." That never happened but our friendship blossomed over the years. The only thing that made me happier than seeing Dusty in the on-deck circle on April 8, 1974, was having him agree to write the foreword of this book fifty years later.

As one of the most successful managers in baseball history, he's virtually certain to follow Hank into the Hall of Fame and I'll be there to cheer him on—perhaps doing double duty as a host for Jay Smith's Sports Travel and Tours, which I have done virtually every year since 2014.

Special thanks as well to Cassidy Lent, Bruce Markusen, and Josh Rawitch at the Hall of Fame; former HOF presidents Jeff Idelson and Tim Mead; and the now-retired guardian of the library's riches Jim Gates, whose wise counsel was always appreciated.

John Thorn, a fellow author whose most recent calling is official historian of Major League Baseball, is always available to answer questions, write forewords, and offer well-considered words. The son of Holocaust survivors, he's a rare baseball personality who thinks before he speaks.

I also appreciate the support of other friends from SABR, the Society for American Baseball Research. A member since 1981, I've attended dozens of annual conferences, with special fondness for the one in Atlanta that coincided with the retirement of the No. 47 uniform worn by Tom Glavine.

That fondness extends to such SABR friends as Evelyn Begley, Mark Drucker, Steve Elsbery, Mark Kanter, David Krell, Howie Siegel, and Paul Vastola.

Thanks also to a long list of baseball friends, including Ron Blomberg and Al Clark, whose autobiographies I co-authored, plus Jim Kaat, Jim Lovell, Art Shamsky, Jeff Torborg, and the myriad of players who participated in the two-dozen baseball theme cruises I created and hosted.

Personal friends who permitted me to root for Hank Aaron rather than Willie, Mickey, or The Duke include Bob Ibach, Bill Jacobowitz, Brian Mullen, Bob Nesoff, Bonnie and Ken Olivenbaum, Bruce and Phyllis Palley, Linda and Sam Rosen, and Wilma Selenfriend.

I am honored to be included in the Ed Lucas Memorial Group, a dinnertime foursome that once included the celebrated blind sportswriter but still retains his spirit and love for the game: David Fenster, Allen Gross, and Allison Lucas (Ed's widow), and myself. And thank you, Chris Lucas, for carrying on your father's legacy as well as his friendship with me.

The cherished memories of Ed Lucas, Mitch Packer, and Sid Lindheim—all best friends at certain points in my life—will always occupy a special place in my heart.

That heart is healthy today thanks to fitness gurus Barry and Kat Rochester, and especially Nancy Whittaker of the Fair Lawn Senior Center, who admits she knows nothing about baseball but keeps me coming back to her Latino Cardio classes anyway.

In closing, no project could be completed without the cooperation and understanding of family, including Phyllis Schlossberg, Samantha Schlossberg, Ali Nolan, Sophie Nolan, and of course Chelsea, who never demanded to be fed or walked when this dog-owner was on deadline.

—**Dan Schlossberg**
Fair Lawn, New Jersey
April 25, 2023

FOREWORD BY DUSTY BAKER

In 1972, my first full season in the major leagues, I was a twenty-three-year-old outfielder with the Atlanta Braves.

Hank Aaron was one of my teammates and Eddie Mathews became our manager in mid-season, so I had plenty of experience to lean on as I was learning the ropes of becoming a major-league player.

One of the things I had to learn right away was how to cope with the media contingent that was growing every day as Hank approached one of the most famous records in sports: Babe Ruth's all-time home run record.

I had to figure out who was good, who was fair, and who was just looking for a headline.

Dan Schlossberg asked me for an interview and came out with the first magazine story about me, although the headline was slightly exaggerated. It read, "Dusty Baker: The Next Hank Aaron."

I appreciated the flattery but knew, even at that young age, that no one could ever fill Hank Aaron's shoes.

I also learned over the years that Dan Schlossberg was going to be one of the top writers around.

More than fifty years later, he is still one of my favorite dudes. Our paths don't cross often, as he lives in the New York area, but I enjoy seeing him and talking baseball at the All-Star Game, World Series, winter meetings, and spring training.

He was covering when I took five different teams to the play-offs: the Giants, Cubs, Reds, Nationals, and Astros. And he always had a smile, a story, or a funny anecdote that brought a smile to my face.

To me, he isn't just a writer. He's a friend.

But he's also an ardent fan of the game and especially of the Atlanta Braves. That is why I am honored he asked me to write the foreword of this book celebrating the 50th anniversary of Hank Aaron breaking Babe Ruth's record.

It's hard to believe fifty years have passed since I was involved in that historic day, on April 8, 1974. In fact, I was in the on-deck circle in the fourth inning at Atlanta Fulton County Stadium when Hank broke the record, connecting for his 715th home run against Al Downing of the Los Angeles Dodgers.

As Hank approached home plate, I stepped aside. The moment was his and I didn't want to do anything that might distract from it.

Darrell Evans, who was on first base, scored ahead of Hank, whose first words to the stadium and television audience were, "I'm just glad it's finally over with."

I had no clue about the magnitude of that night until I got further away from it. It was not only great for baseball, but for America. There were people rooting against him because he was Black, but it also united races all over the world.

Hank was a modest, humble guy. Externally, that's how you're supposed to be but internally he was extremely confident.

Sandy Koufax was the same way. That's what true greatness is about.

Hank had spent the whole winter wondering when or if he would finally make history. And he had to endure a torrent of terrible mail from people who hated the thought that a Black man would wipe out the most hallowed record in sports just because it was owned by Babe Ruth, an American Hero.

Although I am a Black man myself, I grew up in California, but still endured to a far lesser degree than what Hank and my parents' generation endured. I did not have to endure the slights and segregation suffered by Henry Louis Aaron as a native of Mobile, Alabama; a veteran of the Negro Leagues; and the first African American in the Southern League. Spring training in Florida and even some major-league cities were still segregated long after Henry broke into the big leagues in 1954.

It's tough enough to succeed in major-league baseball when the playing field is level. But to face death threats, to require bodyguards, and to have two separate hotel rooms in each city, one of which he slept in under an alias, made it even harder for Hank. And I'm sure it reminded him of his first few years, when the Braves had to find separate quarters for their Black and white players. It was still the same for all of us in my first couple of years in baseball.

Hank didn't talk about the hate mail he received but we knew it was there. He had it in his locker. He would throw it on the floor, and we'd read it when he went to the training room. His behavior was kind of like your parents not bringing their problems home; that's how Hank was with us.

When I got to Chicago years later, I got the same mail. But thanks to the lessons I learned from Hank, I was able to channel that in a positive direction. I got some hate mail here in Texas, too, so it hasn't stopped, though it's probably not as much as it used to be. But I learned a lot from Hank on how to deal with it.

Dan Schlossberg is more than a fan of Hank Aaron; he is especially empathetic because he suffered his share of prejudice as a Jewish American.

When Dan stopped by the visiting manager's office at Yankee Stadium last August, his hat reminded me of that fact. It read, "The Life and Times of Hank Greenberg," the title of a terrific documentary by Aviva Kempner. Not only was Hank Greenberg the original "Hammerin' Hank," but a humanitarian who was influential in helping Jackie Robinson succeed in his difficult rookie year.

Greenberg was playing first base for Pittsburgh in 1947, his last season but Jackie's first, when Robinson reached base for Brooklyn early in the season. Hank said, "Jackie, I had to deal with prejudice and bigotry too. Let me help you get through this."

It's not surprising that the Baseball Hall of Fame has room for two Hammerin' Hanks, whose plaques share the gallery with the one that means the most to me: the one honoring Jackie Robinson.

Jackie and Larry Doby not only ended the color line in baseball but opened the door wide for players like Willie Mays, Ernie Banks, Frank Robinson, Bob Gibson, Rickey Henderson, and of course Hank Aaron.

Hank gave me all kinds of advice about how to behave and carry myself on the field and off. For example, I was once told by him never to mess with St. Louis Cardinals pitcher Bob Gibson. I was told never to stare at him, talk to him, or even smile at him. And if he hit me with a pitch, I was told never to charge the mound, because he was a Golden Gloves boxer. Plus, I'd never have the nerve to do that. I had just watched him strike out 18 Tigers in the 1968 World Series.

I first met Hank in August of 1967, before I ever signed. I had two weeks to go before I would have entered college. The Braves flew my mom and me down to Los Angeles, and I tried out in Dodger Stadium. As a kid, I was a Dodgers fan but had seen Hank, Joe Adcock, and Eddie Mathews hit home runs in a double-header at the old Los Angeles Coliseum.

Hank told my mom if I signed, he would take care of me as if I was his son—and he did just that. I was closer in age to his kids than I was to him. I played jacks with Dorinda, jumped rope with Gaile, and played basketball with Hankie and Lary. At that time, Hank was married to Barbara, sister of farm director (and later GM) Bill Lucas.

Ralph Garr and I came up with the Braves around the same time.

Hank was hard on us. If we were doing something wrong, he would let us know. If he called us boy or hard-headed, we knew he meant business. There were times when he acted like our dad but times when he acted like our uncle or brother.

He taught us when to be cool and when to stand up and be a man. Doing that could be detrimental to your health, especially in those days. I had seen Lester Maddox, George Wallace, and the Freedom Marches on TV and did not want to play in the South, being from California.

But Hank was already there. I remember going to his house and seeing Maynard Jackson, Andrew Young, Ralph David Abernathy, and so many other civil rights leaders. My parents were involved in that, too. Going to the South and being with Hank ended up being the best thing that happened to me.

Hank was big on civil rights. He was not bitter at all. I don't know how he could go through what he went through and not be bitter.

I learned what a giving person Hank was. He gave away scholarships and money through the Hank Aaron Foundation, helping white and Black kids. He treated people as fairly as anybody I ever met. He and my father, both being from the South, went through a lot of changes.

Hank once said, "Do me a favor. Whether you understand what I tell you or not, just retain it. Two, three, or four years from now, it might come to you." And you know what? It still comes back to help me today.

He taught us how to train, how to eat right, and how to handle a day game after a night game. He played racquetball and handball to keep his hands strong. I saw him take a Sunday paper, crumple it up, and hold it in his hands to keep them strong. That must have contributed to his reputation as "a wrist hitter." He also worked on an ice truck as a kid, delivering ice for the ice boxes.

Hank taught us so much about baseball and life. A lot of things I used later in my career came from what he taught me then.

He also taught us a lot about what was coming when we were at the plate. That included a gameplan and theory on how to hit Tom Seaver, how to make him get the ball down, and how to hit Steve Carlton's slider. He could tell by the way you held your bat whether you were going to be a high-ball hitter or low-ball hitter. You had to retain what you learned on the field, or you wouldn't survive.

I once asked Hank who was his toughest pitcher. He said, "You ask too many questions." So I stopped. And then he said,

"Don't you have a question for me?" So I repeated the question and he mentioned Sandy Koufax. Then I asked Sandy who was the toughest hitter for him and he said Bad Henry. That amazed me.

Off the field, Hank was an astute businessman who owned a BMW car dealership, a Church's Chicken franchise, and a Dunkin Donuts. Billye once let me drive his BMW in spring training. Billye was the best thing to happen to Hank after he and Barbara got divorced. That life-changing experience really hurt Hank.

One of the saddest things of my life was the morning of his passing, right before spring training in 2021. I had just taken the job as manager of the Astros. My wife came in and woke me up to tell me.

Hank Aaron was the best person I ever knew and the truest, most honest person I ever knew. He impacted my life, my family, and my world on and off the field. He was a great man. It is my privilege and honor for Dan Schlossberg to ask me to write this foreword.

—**Dusty Baker**
Houston, Texas
August 29, 2023

Dusty Baker was a star outfielder for the Atlanta Braves, Los Angeles Dodgers, and others for 19 years before becoming a major-league manager. In 26 seasons, he won more than 2,000 games, plus three pennants and a World Series, while taking five different teams into the playoffs: the Giants, Cubs, Reds, Nationals, and Astros.

PREFACE BY KEVIN BARNES

I first met Dan Schlossberg in the dugout of Atlanta Stadium when I was the Braves' batboy in 1973.

Dan had come to Atlanta for the last homestand to do research and interviews for a book he was writing on Hank Aaron. I was in the dugout prior to the game. Dan introduced himself and we just started talking.

Dan explained that he was from New Jersey, and that immediately caught my attention. I was born in New York City but grew up in Fort Lee, on the other side of the Hudson, so we immediately had a bond.

He said he'd like to interview me and I said, somewhat sarcastically, "Sure." He said he'd put me in the book and I thought, "Fat chance." But we talked anyway.

Dan said he was a big Hank Aaron fan as well as a big Braves fan, going all the way back to Milwaukee. I told him my favorite player was Mickey Mantle and I went to many games in Yankee Stadium.

Getting a job as a batboy is a dream of many kids growing up, and I was extremely fortunate to be the batboy for the 1973 season. The Braves didn't have a great record, but I have many great memories.

Being around manager Eddie Mathews and players like Hank Aaron, Phil Niekro, Darrell Evans, Dusty Baker, and Davey Johnson—all of whom are either in or have a shot to make the Hall of Fame—plus every other player, coach, and staff member helped me launch a fifty-plus year career in Major League Baseball.

So, in the offseason just prior to the 1974 campaign, I get a copy of *Hammerin' Hank: The Henry Aaron Story*—and find my quotes on Hank.

Now I realize Dan wasn't joking and was a man of his word. Actually, he's a man of many words, as indicated by his forty-one baseball books.

I was there for Home Run 715 to pass Babe Ruth and No. 733, Hank's last with the Braves. I saw Hank many, many times over the years and he was always very friendly—a class act all the way.

I even played softball and batted ahead of Hank once, but that's another story.

Dan has remained a great friend over the years, even though many don't know he was the pitcher for four of my 841 career stickball home runs—including No. 755 and No. 756.

Dan's knuckleball may not be as good as Phil Niekro's was, but Dan can throw a tennis ball with conviction.

That conviction may not always meet with success on the mound, but always meets with his success as a baseball writer.

Dan is certainly well-versed on Braves history and the baseball history of Hank Aaron. As someone who's still writing, I would be hard-pressed to find a person more qualified than Dan to write a book about Hammerin' Hank.

Dan has forged a long career writing about his love for the game of baseball. His books have always been informative and well researched. He's been a fixture at the Winter Meetings, where we once played on the same softball team as Baseball Commissioner Peter Ueberroth, as well as All-Star and World Series games.

Although I've played a great deal of baseball (never with Dan on the field), I know he's had a lot of hits in the press box and in bookstores.

I'm sure he'll hit a home run with this new book on Hank Aaron.

—**Kevin Barnes**
Atlanta, Georgia

[The author wrote this preface on July 21, 2023, fifty years to the day he was batboy for Hank Aaron's 700th home run in Atlanta Stadium.]

INTRODUCTION

Even the heavens are celebrating.

On April 8, 2024—the 50th anniversary of Hank Aaron breaking Babe Ruth's record—a total eclipse occurred over Atlanta. It was just be another sign that Hank Aaron may be gone from earth but never from the imagination of its inhabitants—especially to those who saw him play.

Henry Louis Aaron was the best player I ever saw. And I've been covering baseball since 1969.

Forget Willie, Mickey, and Duke. Had Hank played in New York, or been more flamboyant, Terry Cashman might have written about *him*.

Instead, we have the Ernie Harwell song "Move Over Babe, Here Comes Henry," and more than a dozen Aaron books, including three autobiographies.

But only one—the first one—was written by a journalist who is also an ardent Aaron fan.

That first book, *Hammerin' Hank: The Henry Aaron Story*, was my first, produced for Stadia Sports Publishing in 1974 and in bookstores before he surpassed Babe Ruth's home run total, the most celebrated record in professional sports, on April 8, 1974. He finished his career with 755.

Nobody else has ever hit more—at least not without the suspicion of using performance-enhancing substances.

Barry Bonds hit 762 and won seven MVP awards in the process, but has been barred from the Baseball Hall of Fame by both the beat writers and by the Contemporary Players Era panel, an off-shoot of the old Veterans Committee.

Voters in both groups obviously wondered why Bonds reached the 50-homer plateau only once—in the year he suddenly smacked 73, a single-season standard that still stands. The cloud of suspicion grows darker every year—even fifty years after Aaron beat Ruth.

It's hard to believe a half-century has passed since that historic achievement. It's also hard to believe it happened in the fourth game, in the fourth inning, in the fourth month of a year ending in four, against a pitcher wearing No. 44 by a hitter wearing the exact same numerals.

Although the Monday night game was carried by NBC and the visiting Los Angeles Dodgers, the audio that most frequently accompanies the video is Milo Hamilton's account for Atlanta radio station WSB, then the flagship of the vast Braves radio network.

As the co-author of Milo's autobiography, *Making Airwaves: 60 Years at Milo's Microphone*, he had to fight for the mic that night—but prevailed over Ernie Johnson Sr. as the Braves' lead announcer. Milo's feelings on the matter are included in this book.

So are comments from Eddie Mathews, who combined with Aaron to set the record for home runs by teammates (863); Dusty

Baker, who was in the on-deck circle when Aaron connected; and even Kevin Barnes, who served as Aaron's teenaged batboy at the time but has become a regular presence in the Atlanta press box as a stat man for visiting broadcasters.

My interest in Aaron began in 1957, when my father and I watched the World Series between the Braves and Yankees on our black-and-white Zenith TV. At age nine, my first memories of the game included watching Lew Burdette win three games, including two shutouts, against the powerful Yankees and watching Aaron hit .393 with three home runs.

Burdette won the Chevrolet given to the World Series MVP, but it wouldn't be the first time Aaron was overlooked.

Too quiet, too modest, and too humble, Aaron let his bat speak for him. But his best years came long before the dot.com revolution, accompanied by the advent of cable television and satellite radio, gave baseball access to millions of fans who previously had to rely on newspapers and a weekly publication called *The Sporting News*, which even printed Triple-A box scores.

Aaron lacked the muscle of Mickey Mantle, the flair of Willie Mays, or the swagger of Duke Snider, but finished far ahead of that trio in the record books.

He was an All-Star a record 25 times in 23 seasons because the major leagues played two All-Star games a year, from 1959–1962, to raise money for the players' pension fund.

He had more runs scored, runs batted in, total bases, and extra-base hits than anyone in baseball history—including The Babe himself—and more home runs hit without the taint of steroids.

He survived segregation in the Jim Crow South during spring training, a torrent of hate mail from fans who couldn't bear the thought of a Black man breaking a white hero's record, and rejection by writers who voted him only one Most Valuable Player trophy when he should have had four.

Then there were those nine so-called sportswriters who left Aaron's name off their 10-man ballots for the Baseball Hall of Fame. *Nine!* And that was *before* anyone was protesting the exclusion of Pete Rose for allegedly gambling on the game.

By 1982, the year Aaron was inducted, he had finally won some respect both in baseball circles and from baseball fans at large.

I should not have been surprised that nobody believed me when I told my classmates in Passaic, New Jersey that Hank Aaron was going to break Babe Ruth's record. Ask any of them: I made the prediction *ten years before it actually happened!*

I bragged about Aaron so much that my high school friends called me "Hank" when they weren't calling me "Vince," since I also emulated Vin Scully's habit of calling everyone fans.

In driveway stickball games, we made up batting orders and pretended to be real players. Already an avid Braves fan, I tried harder when pretending to be Hank Aaron. And I always listed him third or fourth—the best spots in the order.

A model of consistency, Aaron never hit more than 47 home runs in a season but always seemed to hit at least 30. He hit 47 once, and matched his uniform No. 44 four times. He also maintained amazing physical condition, something his brother Tommie couldn't do, and wound up on the disabled list only once, when he broke his leg sliding in September of his rookie year of 1954.

Had he been with better teams, Hank Aaron might have earned more recognition. But he reached the World Series only twice, in 1957 and 1958, and narrowly missed a third chance when the Milwaukee Braves dropped a best-of-three pennant playoff to the 1959 Los Angeles Dodgers.

Hank made it to the very first National League Championship Series in 1969, but the favored Braves fell victim to the red-hot New York Mets, who swept a playoff that could have been best-of-three.

Variously described as a wrist hitter, a guess hitter, and a man so relaxed that he looked like he was sleeping between pitches, he was a modest but muscular man whose 6-foot, 180-pound frame hardly looked intimidating . . . until he swung the bat.

Hank Aaron had all five tools: he hit for average, hit for power, and could run, field, and throw. He won three Gold Gloves for fielding excellence, enjoyed a 30/30 season, and won all three legs of the Triple Crown in multiple seasons—just not at the same time.

Missing a Triple Crown and failing to hit for the cycle were the only disappointments in a long career that began when he boarded a train in Alabama with a sandwich in his hand and $2 in his pocket.

Were Hank Aaron around today, he would no doubt own the Braves franchise. His top salary of $240,000 would be tip money today, when more than a dozen players earn more than $30 million a year.

In addition to his exploits on the field, Hank Aaron was also a hero in civilian clothes. An outspoken champion of civil rights, he formed friendships with presidents and civil rights leaders. His quiet but steady excellence won him legions of admirers not only at home but also when the Braves visited other cities.

He got so much fan mail that the US Postal Service once gave him a medal as the person who received the most mail in the

United States. Though the tenor of letters was overwhelmingly supportive, more than a few malcontents threatened the lives of the slugger and his family, forcing the team to provide him with bodyguards and housing separate from the team during road trips.

Talk about irony: a man who once couldn't stay with the team because of segregation that lingered long after Jackie Robinson integrated the majors now couldn't stay with the team because he was a Black man pursuing a white man's record.

Like Robinson, who broke the color line seven years before Aaron reached the majors, Hank Aaron burned inside but kept his cool, never giving the naysayers more ammunition. Though disappointed that he didn't realize his ambition to be a manager or even a general manager, he eschewed conflict and controversy as much as humanly possible.

He aged nicely, establishing widespread respect as a humanitarian, civil rights advocate, and successful businessman—dabbling in everything from restaurants to car dealerships in addition to Cable News Network and various positions with the Braves. He had tough decisions to make, even cutting son Lary and future Atlanta manager Brian Snitker, but always proved the epitome of grace under pressure.

He knew presidents, movie stars, and other celebrities who seemed truly delighted to befriend him.

In fact, I was interviewing him in the Atlanta clubhouse after a game in September 1973 when the Governor of Georgia stopped by to say hello.

Aaron excused himself and shook hands with a smiling Jimmy Carter while I waited to resume the interview. A picture of that event circulated on MLB.com early in the 2023 season.

The very next day, Carter announced he was running for president—an event the *Atlanta Journal-Constitution* headlined JIMMY CARTER IS RUNNING FOR *WHAT?*

Hank Aaron could have run for president himself. I would have voted for him.

—**Dan Schlossberg**
Fair Lawn, New Jersey
April 17, 2023

CHAPTER 1
A NIGHT TO REMEMBER

In the long and storied history of baseball, certain dates are carved in stone.

Lou Gehrig called himself "the luckiest man on the face of the earth" on July 4, 1939.

Jackie Robinson broke the nefarious color barrier on April 15, 1947.

Bobby Thomson hit his "shot heard 'round the world" on October 3, 1951.

Roger Maris hit his 61st home run ten years later, on October 1, 1961.

Then there was April 8, 1974, the date a humble man from a mediocre team far from the nation's media capitals devoured the most hallowed record in sports.

Hank Aaron brought many qualities to the dance: the elegance of Lou Gehrig, the passion of Jackie Robinson, the timing of Bobby Thomson, and the modesty of Roger Maris.

With an air of expectancy hanging over the stadium, along with enough cumulonimbus clouds to exacerbate the anxiety of the locals, the Braves held a 45-minute pregame tribute to

Aaron's career. Anticipating a packed house, the normal police presence of seventeen was nearly tripled.

Once the game finally started, Aaron drew a walk in his first at-bat. The crowd booed.

And then it happened.

In the fourth inning of the fourth game, in the fourth month of a year that ended in four, Henry Louis Aaron, wearing No. 44 for the Atlanta Braves, hit a home run against Al Downing, a pitcher wearing the same numerals for the Los Angeles Dodgers. With a 1-0 count, Aaron picked on a high fastball as Darrell Evans scored from first base, while Dusty Baker from the on-deck circle and Davey Johnson in the hole watched history unfold just a few feet away.

Bill Buckner, playing left field for Los Angeles that night, made a valiant leap but came up empty as the ball sailed into the Braves' bullpen and into the mitt of relief pitcher Tom House. "Seven hundred home runs," said Buckner, who would have his own date with history twelve years later. "I couldn't hit 700 home runs in batting practice for three straight months."

The stadium clock read 9:07 p.m. Eastern Standard Time.

After an eleven-minute ceremony to celebrate the momentous home run, a shell-shocked Downing couldn't regain his command. He walked both Baker and Johnson, ending his evening.

Downing, who had never lost to the Braves in nine previous starts (going 5–0), had been trying to keep the fateful pitch down. He was unsuccessful in that attempt.

"I didn't want to be the guy who gave up the home run," he said before the game. "No pitcher likes to give up a home run at any time. It could cost him the ballgame."

It was Aaron's 2,967th game and 11,294th at-bat.

Among the millions who watched the telecast was Don Money, an infielder who had played against Aaron and would soon become his teammate. "I couldn't help but notice the way Hank accepted his place in baseball history," he wrote in his book *The Man Who Made Milwaukee Famous.*

"As he was shown rounding the bases, my thoughts went back to the times I had seen his home run trot when I was with the Phillies," continued Money. "There was no difference. He circled the Atlanta infield on the night he made history the same way he had done it when I was a member of the opposition. Hank made his way around the bases deliberately, without showmanship. He went into the record book with the same style and class he had exhibited throughout his career. That meant something to me."

Aaron's blow tied the game, 3–3, and set the stage for the Braves to have their way against newly entered reliever Mike Marshall (who would go on to win the Cy Young Award after pitching 208 relief innings and 106 games, both records for relief pitchers). But not that night, when the Braves batted around in the fourth inning before Marshall, an offseason kinesiology professor at Michigan State, finally slammed the door.

Celebrating in the dugout was manager Eddie Mathews, who had combined with Aaron to hit a record 863 home runs for the Braves during the time in which they were teammates. He would not complete the season as manager—even leaving when the team had a winning record—but would always be remembered as Aaron's friend and protector.

For Aaron, it wasn't just *any* home run, but his 715th, placing him one ahead of Babe Ruth on the all-time list. It not only defied the force of gravity, but the course of logic.

A Black man born fourteen years before Jackie Robinson's courageous one-man stand against a century of bigotry, Aaron began as an infielder who batted cross-handed for a barnstorming Negro Leagues team called the Indianapolis Clowns, baseball's answer to the Harlem Globetrotters.

The barrage of racial epithets, segregation, and separation he battled in his early years morphed into a tirade of threats and hate mail as his steady approach to Ruth's record attracted the attention not only of the sports press but also mainstream news organizations.

He answered his detractors with a stoic demeanor that made him seem calm on the outside even though the hurt had to be enormous. Early in his career, he had to stay and eat in separate facilities during spring training because the Braves were stationed in Florida before the Supreme Court's landmark *Brown v. Board of Education* eliminated "separate but equal" public schools for Black students.

Once the season started, things were not always better—especially in slow-to-integrate places like St. Louis, Cincinnati, and Philadelphia.

At least young Aaron was playing half his schedule in Wisconsin, where the fans and media made him feel welcome even when the ballpark didn't. Milwaukee County Stadium was not especially conducive to the long ball and the climate was often cold and windy, especially in April and September.

After a 13-year baseball marriage that began with a euphoric honeymoon, new owners decided to try the virgin territory of the American South. Aaron, well aware of the burgeoning civil rights movement, was not happy about it. He had already integrated the all-white South Atlantic League in the minors and retained bitter memories of that experience.

But then he discovered the hitter-friendly dimensions of his new home ballpark, Atlanta Stadium, and also learned that the city's altitude was the highest in the majors at the time of the team's transfer (two expansion teams, the Colorado Rockies and Arizona Diamondbacks, later outranked Atlanta in feet above sea level).

After hitting just 13 home runs as a rookie in 1954, and relative handfuls in subsequent seasons, Aaron changed his approach at the plate, becoming a dead-pull hitter.

He hit a combined 56 home runs in his last two Milwaukee campaigns, then suddenly, in 1966—his first year in Atlanta— he hit 44 with 127 RBIs.

Remarkably consistent, he never hit more than 47 in a season. By the time he reached his fortieth birthday in 1974, he had 713 home runs—one short of Ruth's record—and had led his league in home runs and runs batted in four times each.

Yet getting to No. 715 seemed to take forever.

One year earlier, with the record in sight, Aaron finished with 40 home runs—the last time he would reach that plateau.

Aaron had hoped to reach the record during the final days of the 1973 season, but both the weather and the opposing pitchers refused to cooperate.

Neither proved to be as formidable an obstacle, however, as baseball commissioner Bowie Kuhn.

With the Braves determined to host the historic home run in Atlanta, which had been starved for attendance, Mathews announced he would bench Aaron for the season-opening, three-game series that pitted the Braves against the Reds in Cincinnati.

Kuhn insisted otherwise and Mathews, not one to let anyone dictate his lineup, issued a loud and passionate protest. An uneasy peace was reached only after Kuhn threatened to punish both the manager and the ballclub.

In the meantime, the media had a field day, with most—including New York icons Dave Anderson and Dick Young—protesting Atlanta's decision to "rest" its best player in the second game of the season. On the other hand, *The Sporting News* reported that Stan Musial once sat in Chicago so that he could get his 3,000th hit at home in St. Louis. So there was precedent.

Mathews, the only man to play for the Braves in Boston, Milwaukee, and Atlanta, as well as the only man to play for, coach, and manage the team, relented begrudgingly, agreeing to play the forty-year-old Aaron twice—in the Thursday opener and Sunday finale against the Reds. At the same time, everyone connected with the Braves found themselves in the untenable position of rooting against the team's best player.

The PR department had ordered 50,000 copies of placards that read I WAS THERE WHEN HANK HIT 714 and I WAS THERE WHEN HANK HIT 715.

That didn't stop Aaron from tying Ruth on the first pitch he saw, in the first inning on April 4, with a 3-1 count and two men on base against Jack Billingham. It was the first time in his career that he had homered on Opening Day.

The pitcher's wife came over to congratulate Billye Aaron. "She made a special effort to congratulate Henry and to speak to us even though her husband had thrown the home run ball," Billye remembered. "I really thought that was nice."

The blast even prompted a congratulatory telegram from Babe Ruth's widow, Clare. "She wished me happiness and all the luck in the world," Aaron said.

He couldn't connect again, however, sitting out the second game and going 0-for-3 in the finale against Clay Kirby, thus allowing Atlanta to prepare a raucous welcome for the soon-to-be home run king.

He didn't take long to deliver.

"I read I wasn't trying my best during that last game in Cincinnati," said Aaron, who tantalized the fans with a long fly ball for one of the three outs he made in the Sunday finale. "I'd just like to say that I have never stepped onto a field when I did not do my level best."

He wasn't done. Given a national stage by NBC, which broadcast the game on its network as part of *Monday Night Baseball,* Aaron told viewers, "I'm just happy it's over. I feel now I can relax, my teammates can relax, and I can go on and have a great year.

"This is something I wanted. For years I felt I was slighted by awards and things like that. I worked very hard to get to where I am although I never thought five years ago I would ever be in this position.

"Now I can consider myself one of the best. Maybe not *the* best because a lot of great ones have played this game—DiMaggio, Mays, Jackie Robinson. I think I can fit in there somewhere."

The ball fit in somewhere, too—inside the glove of a young left-handed Atlanta reliever named Tom House. After fighting his bullpen teammates for the baseball, he bolted through the bullpen gate and onto the field, pushing through the mob at home plate so that he could present the prize to Aaron. The bespectacled reliever, who later became a celebrated pitching coach, must have caught a little pixie dust with the ball as he went on to have his best season in 1974.

Aaron accepted hugs from his parents, Estella and Herbert Aaron, and new wife Billye, weeping from the joy of the moment but the exhaustion of the wait. Billye gave Henry a hard and long kiss caught by the national television cameras.

In the ceremony that followed, majority owner Bill Bartholomay gave Aaron a plaque, Georgia Governor Jimmy Carter presented him with vanity license plate HLA 715, and Hall of Famer Monte Irvin handed the slugger a $3,000 gold watch lined with diamonds. But Bowie Kuhn—after causing considerable commotion over Aaron's playing status in the opening road series—made himself scarce, sending Irvin to represent his office. When Irvin included Kuhn's name in his congratulatory speech, the negative reaction of the 53,775 Atlanta fans was both vociferous and predictable.

Kuhn, who chose Cleveland's Wahoo Club over Aaron's historic moment, did at least send a wire. So did Ted Williams, Roy Campanella, Joe Louis, and thousands of adoring fans. Aaron even received a telephone call from the White House, although Richard M. Nixon had many other things on his mind in the spring of '74.

Commercial offers—including one from the Oh! Henry candy bar company—also poured in.

For Aaron, the outpouring was overwhelming. "The average person doesn't know what a nightmare this has been," he told reporters after the game. "The same old questions, the controversy. I'll enjoy it all a little later."

Through it all, Aaron tried to keep his cool—even when one female reporter asked, "Mr. Aaron, can you tell us whether you bat right-handed or left-handed?"

All she had to do was watch the pre-game "This Is Your Life" presentation focused around Aaron. It included an enormous map pinpointing places Aaron played, from his hometown of Mobile to his minor-league stops in Jacksonville and Eau Claire. Friends and family took part, popping up as various destinations were announced.

Fans cheered as Aaron walked through a gauntlet of bats held by a bevy of local beauty queens, brought in by publicist Lee Walburn and his eager and innovative assistant Bob Hope. Nobody seemed to mind the damp and dreary weather conditions, though some worried that the heavens might open before the game became official, wiping out the historic home run.

Aaron's quest began in 1971, when he surprised both himself and the baseball world by hitting 47 home runs in 139 games at the ripe old athletic age of thirty-seven. It was the first of four straight seasons in which his playing time would diminish because of arthritis and other nagging injuries, but he led the league with a .669 slugging percentage, the best of his career.

"When I hit 47 home runs, I began to think I could break Ruth's record," he said. "I started to swing more consciously for homers in 1972 than ever before in my career. The fact is that I had a chance to equal or surpass perhaps the most respected record on the baseball books. I'd be foolish not to do everything I could to accomplish the feat."

Trying for home runs didn't necessarily help. Because a player strike wiped out the start of the season, Aaron lost his spring training edge and started slowly, with five singles in his first 50 at-bats. By season's end, his production had taken a nose-dive. He finished with an uncharacteristic .265 average (the lowest of his then-19-year career) and 34 homers while trying to save his arm by playing first base, but Aaron knew he still could catch Ruth if he could regroup for at least one more season.

"I had a tendency to get tired that year," he remembered. "I was overtired a couple of times and it took me a while to bounce back."

When Eddie Mathews replaced Lum Harris as manager during the '72 season, the first thing he did was work out a schedule of regular rest days for Aaron. But it was too little too late.

Back in the outfield for 1973, Aaron's bat showed new signs of life. But so did his mail box: he received 930,000 letters, earning a special plaque from the US Postal Service as the person who received the most mail in the United States. Unfortunately, anonymous bigots and racists sent far too many of those messages.

"The Ruth chase should have been the greatest period of my life," Aaron said years later, "but it was the worst. I couldn't believe there was so much hatred in people."

For his own protection, Aaron ate separately and stayed apart from his teammates on the road—just as he had early in his career when towns and cities were slow to integrate. He received much-needed security protection not only from the hate-mongers but also from the media horde that grew larger every day.

"The pressure was enormous," said Mathews, once the lefty half of the best 1-2 punch in baseball history. "No other athlete could have handled the situation as well as Hank. The club gave him a private secretary, a private limousine and hired a police detective. We had to hide him in hotels under assumed names, sneaking him in and out. It was hairy but he handled it in stride."

Unlike many other athletes, Aaron prospered under pressure. The more there was, the better he performed.

"I am better when the pressure is on and there is motivation," he said in 1973. "Breaking Ruth's record is motivation. I am happy to be in a position where I can break it."

The pressure intensified after Aaron hit a Ken Brett pitch for his 700th home run on July 21. The Braves retrieved the ball by offering 700 silver dollars to whomever retrieved it; a senior from Westminster High School turned out to be the lucky fan.

Bowie Kuhn, however, was not there—even though Aaron was only the second man in baseball history to hit 700 home runs. Nor did the commissioner send a congratulatory wire, a snub that irritated Aaron. But he went on with his relentless "Race for the Record."

Roger Maris, who had his own race with Ruth thirteen years earlier, came to Atlanta hoping to witness history in the making. "The pressure was terrific—mentally much more than physically," Maris said of his successful bid to become the single-season home run king. "You have no idea what it was like to put up with something like that for two months. People around you all the time. You can't eat, you can't sleep, you can't even think. I wish I had done it in my last year.

"Hank will learn that the only time he's going to get any relief is when he's out on the field," Maris said. "He will never be able to enjoy himself either before or after games. He'll never be able to relax—that's how intense the demands on his time will be."

Aaron admitted he had constant requests for interviews and invitations for banquets. "People were always asking me to make public appearances," he said. "I just didn't have enough time to satisfy everyone. I needed some time to myself—like anyone else—to relax physically and mentally."

Even Clara Ruth, widow of the Babe, complained about the demands on her time. "I just want some peace of mind," she said in the late summer of 1973. "Everywhere I go, there are the same old questions. I'm fed up with it. And I don't think it's good taste for me to intrude."

By the end of the '73 season, Aaron was *thisclose* to "The Record."

On Tuesday, September 25, future Braves broadcaster Don Sutton outdueled Phil Niekro, 5–1, in a battle of eventual 300-game winners as Aaron went 0-for-4. But he did hit a long drive to dead center late in the game. "When you've hit 712," he said, "you know when the ball is likely to go out of the park."

The next night, in hot and muggy conditions, Aaron went 1-for-4 and knocked in two runs. But his foul pop fly ended the game when he failed to connect on a fastball right down the middle. He had been guessing curve.

Then the weather intervened. With the field getting drenched and the Thursday getaway game of no importance to either the Dodgers or the Braves, the umpires faced an easy decision.

"When a game is rained out like this," Aaron said afterward, "it hurts—especially in a park where you're comfortable and you know you can hit home runs."

Vin Scully, the poetic Dodgers broadcaster, added, "Aaron has hit more home runs than anyone alive. Now the Braves are going to see if he can walk on water."

Jimmy Carter, who attended many Braves games, brought fellow governor Sherman Tribbett of Delaware into the clubhouse for a visit. "He came all the way down here just to see you play," the Georgia governor told Aaron, "and it had to rain."

All of a sudden, Aaron had just two games left to hit two homers for a tie or three to break the record. It wouldn't be easy.

"I can do it," said Aaron, noting that he had done it before, "but it just isn't likely."

After a rare day off Friday, the Braves reconvened for a season-ending, two-game set against the Houston Astros, then a National League team managed by former Ruth teammate Leo Durocher.

Their scheduled pitchers were a pair of left-handers, Jerry Reuss and Dave Roberts. Both had surrendered Aaron homers earlier that season.

In the fifth inning, Aaron pounced on a slow curve from Reuss, sending it over the fence in left-center field. The numerals 713 lit up on the Atlanta Stadium scoreboard long before the slugger completed his circuit of the bases.

That home run was Aaron's 40th, allowing him to join Darrell Evans and Davey Johnson as the first trio of teammates to have simultaneous 40-homer seasons (the 2023 Atlanta Braves did it with Matt Olson, Ronald Acuna Jr., and Marcell Ozuna, while the Colorado Rockies did it twice before that). It was the first 40-homer season for both of the younger men but Aaron graciously brought them into his nightly post-game press conference.

Even with the weather still dreary the following day, time was running out for the challenger. But Roberts, the Houston starter, was ready to take him on.

"My job is to get everybody out and that's just what I'll try to do," said the sinkerballer. "I'd rather be a nobody in baseball forever than go down as an immortal because I served one of the big ones to Henry. He got his 712th off me in Houston the other night and that made me mad because it was a three-run job that beat us."

Aaron said later that Roberts threw only one strike during his four at-bats, but he still managed three singles against him, bringing his average up to .301. With his legs getting stronger as the weather warmed, he hit .387 after the July 24 All-Star Game in Kansas City. But he was still one short of tying "The Record"— just as a Georgia State University computer had predicted.

"I refused to believe the computer," he said, "but evidently, it was right. I went into today's game determined to hit a home run and it just didn't work out that way."

By that time, the Braves were using "Aaron balls" specially marked with invisible ink for authentication purposes. But that made it harder to hit one, rather than easier, as pitchers were constantly reminded whenever Aaron came up to bat.

"I was not always thinking 'home run' when I stepped to the plate," he said. "I was concentrating on getting a hit, trying to win the game. If a home run was needed, then I thought it was my duty to try and get it. First you play baseball, then you play to win, and then you go for home runs. The understanding of the fans is important."

For Aaron, the worst part of the "Race with Ruth" was the long winter between baseball seasons.

"I think I've slowed down," he said as the 1973 season wore down to its final days. "You notice it most after a hard night game, especially when you have to go 12 innings and make a lot of throws and putouts. You notice it at the plate when you foul off pitches you should have hit out. In the field, some balls I should have caught dropped in. And sometimes going from first to third, I got tired. Baseball is a young man's game. When you reach thirty-five or thirty-six and you're still having good seasons, you're really fortunate."

For six months, Aaron wondered whether he would even live to take another crack at the record. He was not only concerned about the crackpots but also about his own health, knowing that his forty-year-old body was barking in certain spots, including his neck, knees, and shoulder. Cold weather made things worse, the knee had to be drained regularly, and the slugger consulted two orthopedics who suggested surgery. He would later need glasses, but not yet. And his wrists—his main calling card—were still working.

That winter, Aaron thought about his future in the game, since he did not intend to sign a new contract with the Braves after his current one expired. His long-standing ambition of finding an executive or managerial position—something with the authority to make decisions—had never waned. But the Braves weren't offering anything that tempted him.

"There were times I didn't know if I could go on," Aaron admitted. "But I always did."

He did take a long-awaited fishing trip on his 27-foot-long yacht *Dorinda*, named for his daughter, but he thought about the baseball season to come. After all, how could he not?

"It's been tiresome talking about Babe Ruth," he admitted. "I can't recall a day this year or the last part of last year when I did not hear his name. I would like to get it over with but I'm not going up there and press for home runs.

"I'm much more worried about the pitchers who are trying to prevent me from breaking the record than I am about the people who are going to write and talk about it."

The tumult began again the minute spring training began in 1974. The Braves trained at West Palm Beach Municipal Stadium and played exhibition games mainly designed to get players ready for the regular season. The unofficial season lasted a month but Aaron, like most veterans, was not included in games that required long bus rides—even though almost every opposing team wanted to honor him with a Hank Aaron Day in their ballpark.

With just weeks to go before Opening Day, Aaron and Mathews agreed to pose for a picture outside the batting cage. That picture appears in this book.

With spring training finally over, the Braves flew into the Cincinnati airport—which is actually located in Kentucky—a day before the opener so they could work out at Riverfront Stadium. Aaron was ready to renew the assault on Ruth's record . . . but Mother Nature had other plans.

A wave of tornadoes decimated Xenia, Ohio, 50 miles from the ballpark, killing three-dozen people and causing $15 million in damage. Cincinnati didn't escape unscathed, allowing Aaron to actually see a tornado for the first time in his life. To him, it was more frightening than an inside fastball from Bob Gibson. "It was really something," he said.

The twisters proved to be a harbinger of things to come.

The Braves, hoping to host the history-making event in Atlanta, initially announced Aaron would not play in the three-game Cincinnati series that opened the 1974 season.

Kuhn would have none of it. He ordered the team to play Aaron against the Reds.

"We received a message from the Commissioner," said Mathews in response to reporters' questions about playing Aaron on the road. "He has unlimited powers to impose very serious penalties on individuals and the ballclub itself. For the first time, I realized that those penalties are not only fines but also suspensions and other threats to the franchise."

The issue was resolved with a compromise: the Braves would use Aaron twice in the three-game series—matching the usual schedule for a forty-year-old star on the decline.

Aaron's response? "I believe the Braves had a right to promote the only thing going for them right now," he said, "but I don't want to get involved in the Commissioner's decision. I think there is too much fuss over it."

After Aaron homered in the Thursday opener, he sat Saturday, then went hitless in three at-bats Sunday. Friday was a scheduled day off to protect against an Opening Day rainout.

"A week from now we're all going to be laughing about this thing," Mathews said Saturday, "but today has been a little hectic. Right now it feels like World War III. Managers have gone through a whole year and not had a day like I had today."

Aaron agreed. "We obeyed the Commissioner," he said. "I'm happy and I hope everybody's happy. I just hope tomorrow night it will all be over with and things can get back to normal. It's been quite a week and I'm glad to be going home."

The Braves declared April 8 "Hank Aaron Night," and invited numerous celebrities, including Pearl Bailey, who sang the National Anthem, and Sammy Davis Jr., in addition to Jimmy Carter. But neither Bowie Kuhn nor Vice President Gerald Ford, who had witnessed the record-tying home run in Cincinnati, were in attendance.

The slugger seemed relieved rather than joyful. "I'm glad I didn't break the record on the road," he said, "but it wasn't for any lack of effort. Some people wondered if I had deliberately *not* hit a home run, which was both stupid and insulting. I had too much pride in my ability and too much respect for the integrity of the game to make an out on purpose."

Aaron didn't wait long to break the tie.

According to Darrell Evans, who scored ahead of Aaron's historic clout, "I feel like he was chosen to break the record. No one else could have handled the situation so well, with such class and quiet dignity."

Evans viewed Aaron as a superstar who was almost anonymous. "We knew Hank well, what he meant to us and how exciting it was," the third baseman said, "but many fans had no idea who he was."

The national broadcast of the big game helped.

Vin Scully called it for the Dodgers, Curt Gowdy for NBC, and Milo Hamilton for Atlanta's powerful flagship WSB radio.

Hamilton almost missed his chance. He did the six o'clock sports report for WSB-TV Channel 2, sped to the ballpark through rush-hour traffic, did the pre-game show, and hosted the pre-game ceremony.

"George Plimpton tried all winter to get me to tell him what I was going to say," said Hamilton, whose career stretched six decades, "but I honestly didn't know. Spontaneity was my strong suit. I didn't want to make it sound contrived."

Hamilton avoided his trademark "Holy Toledo" call. "It was not my moment, it was Hank's," he said. He had also broadcast Aaron's first home run as a visiting announcer with the 1954 St. Louis Cardinals.

"I never thought he would become such a slugger," he said. "As good a hitter as Aaron was in Atlanta, until he announced for the first time in 1972 that he was going after the record, I don't think anyone really thought about it. Everybody thought Babe Ruth's record was there to stay."

To this day, Hamilton's heartfelt call is often paired with the home run video. Aaron eventually left the game early, yielding to the younger, faster Rowland Office as a defensive replacement.

After the game, Mathews kept reporters at bay. He closed the clubhouse to give Aaron time to celebrate with his teammates.

"I locked the door to give us a half-hour with just the team and the families—the wives and the kids," said the manager. "I wanted to let Hank have a chance to shift gears and just enjoy the moment. I climbed up on a table and gave a little talk about Hank, what he had accomplished and how much he had meant to me. After that we had some champagne and let the press come in. Once they came in, I *really* caught hell. The players were all laughing—they loved to see me catch hell."

The next day, Aaron told Dusty Baker he had been celebrating all night. And he told Joe Durso of *The New York Times* that he was wiped.

"The average person can't realize what a nightmare this has been," he said. "The last ten days of last season, all winter, spring training, right up until today. Now I'm just tired. Not let down—just tired. I'm beat. I'll play tomorrow but not tonight."

For Henry Louis Aaron, there would not be many tomorrows left on the field. The rest of the '74 season, his last as a player for the Braves, turned into a farewell tour. He had already stated his intention to retire.

When the team went to Los Angeles early in the season, Dodger third baseman Ron Cey walked into the Braves clubhouse to see him.

"I had two posters and two baseballs that I wanted to have him sign," Cey wrote in his 2023 book *Penguin Power*. "I didn't know exactly how I was going to do that so I just decided to take the bull by the horns. I walked across the field into the Braves dugout and up into the clubhouse. Aaron wasn't at his locker but when he got there, he saw me and smiled. I said, 'I'm not going anywhere until these balls and posters are signed.' He said, 'No problem,' and was great about it."

Before, during, and after his reign as the home run king, Henry Aaron left his imprint with every autograph he signed, every hand he shook, and every person he met.

Even Don Drysdale, the fearsome side-armer who yielded more Aaron home runs than any other pitcher, had his number. After The Hammer hit the home run that tied Babe Ruth, Drysdale sent a wire that read, "You'd be 17 short without me!"

Aaron vs. Downing
Hank Aaron hit two home runs in eight at-bats against Al Downing the year before hitting No. 715 against him.

Aaron's Victims
The list of pitchers who surrendered Hank Aaron home runs includes an infielder doing mop-up duty, Johnny O'Brien of the Pittsburgh Pirates; a pitcher-turned-policeman named Corky Valentine; a congressman, Vinegar Bend Mizell; and a U.S. Senator, Jim Bunning.

After the Homer
In his first at-bat aftter hitting the fourth-inning homer that broke Babe Ruth's record, Hank Aaron heard encouragement from

Ralph Garr, one of several who called him Superman:"C'mon, Super, go break Hank Aaron's record!"

Touching the Bases
To make No. 715 official, Hank Aaron had to touch all the bases. Ralph Garr helped, grabbing Aaron's right leg and setting it down on home plate.

First Pitch
Hank Aaron's father Herbert, Sr. threw out the ceremonial first pitch before the home game in which he broke Babe Ruth's record on April 8, 1974.

CHAPTER 2

BABE'S SHADOW

The day after Henry Aaron was born, on February 5, 1934, Babe Ruth celebrated his thirty-ninth birthday.

He would hit just 22 home runs that year and six more at age forty a year later before retiring as both a ballplayer and a living legend—partially the product of a prolific print media that seized every opportunity to exploit the Ruth mystique in search of a headline.

Other than their uncanny proximity on the Zodiac, the two men were almost polar opposites. Ruth was a burly white man from Baltimore, while Aaron was a svelte but muscular Black man from Mobile, Alabama.

Both were born into poverty, but their adult lives were dramatically different.

Neither had a sparkling debut, with Ruth yielding to a pinch-hitter in his 1914 bow as a pitcher with the Boston Red Sox and Aaron taking an 0-for-5 collar for the Milwaukee Braves against the Cincinnati Reds on April 13, 1954.

Ruth began as a left-handed pitcher whose ability to hit with power not only defined him as a player but effectively ended the

Dead Ball Era, which had been dominated by bunting, stealing bases, executing hit-and-run plays, and manufacturing runs. So many fans flocked to see the bombastic Ruth that his Yankees escaped from the Polo Grounds, where they were tenants of the New York Giants, to build their own ballpark on the Bronx side of the Harlem River.

"The House That Ruth Built" had a notoriously short right-field wall—perfect for the swings of Ruth and Lou Gehrig, left-handed hitters listed third and fourth in the Yankees lineup.

From 1926–1932, Ruth never hit less than .323 or fewer than 41 home runs in a season.

He ate up opposing pitchers, but also had an enormous appetite for wine, women, and song. Teammate Waite Hoyt once joked that if someone sawed Ruth in two, half the concessions of Yankee Stadium would fall out.

Before Jackie Robinson integrated the majors in 1947, young Hank Aaron never thought about Babe Ruth, a white man playing a sport barred to Black men.

"Why would I read about a man playing a game I couldn't get into at the time?" he said.

Only years after Ruth died in 1948 did his shadow descend over Aaron's world like the silhouette of a stout Alfred Hitchcock fitting into its framed outline at the start of his televised mystery hour, *Alfred Hitchcock Presents*.

Aaron became the tortoise chasing Ruth's hare. Slow and steady but amazingly consistent, he passed such milestones as his 500th home run in 1968 and 600th just three years later, in 1971, when he hit a career-high 47 in just 139 games. That performance started tongues wagging.

Comparisons were inevitable.

The 6-foot, 180-pound Aaron worked out, watched his weight, and maintained a low profile. He hit line-drive home runs, as opposed to the long, sweeping curves synonymous with Ruth.

Modest and humble to a fault, Aaron avoided the controversy that seemed to envelop Ruth like a low-hanging cloud. Though he never hit more than 47 home runs in a season, Ruth topped 50 four times, including seasons of 54 in 1920, 59 in 1921, and 60 in 1927.

Unlike Aaron years later, however, Ruth wasn't chasing someone else's record—only his own.

"He had to be the greatest power-hitter, the greatest player," Stan Musial once said of Ruth, his boyhood idol. "He was good enough to pitch and bat fourth, like the star of a high school team."

On the other hand, Musial noted that pitchers lasted longer—even when tired—in Ruth's day, giving hitters the advantage of seeing them four or five times per game and seeing fastballs of reduced velocity late in games.

Ballparks were also smaller when Ruth played, giving him another advantage in the power sweepstakes, Musial said. He added that Aaron had to face such standout Black pitchers as Bob Gibson and Ferguson Jenkins while Ruth faced white pitchers exclusively during his pre-integration career.

Because he was a pitcher first, Ruth had far fewer at-bats than Aaron, enabling him to rank first in home runs per 100 times at bat over the course of his career (8.5).

A left-hander who posted a 94–46 record and 2.28 ERA, he won 23 games in 1916 and 24 in 1917, then set postseason records for shutout innings in the World Series (29). During ten

World Series appearances, Ruth went 3–0 as a pitcher and hit 15 home runs—including one in 1932 that he allegedly predicted by pointing to the stands prior to Charlie Root's pitch.

That was typical for Ruth, known for his camel-hair coat, ever-present cigar, broad smile, and snappy roadster. A carouser who entertained both teammates and women on long train rides between cities, Ruth never seemed to need much rest. He even found time for golf, winning more awards on the links than he ever did on the diamond.

In his book *Super Stars of Baseball*, Bob Broeg wrote that Ruth's gargantuan appetite could include a breakfast of four eggs, a porterhouse steak, fried potatoes, toast, and a pint of bourbon. Between games of a doubleheader, it might be a quart of pickled eels prepared by Lou Gehrig's mom, plus a pint of chocolate ice cream.

Aaron, by contrast, was a staunch conservative. A fan of Polynesian food, he frequented Trader Vic's, sometimes had a pre-game pork chop at a friend's home, and could down a beer or two after a night game. Not a hard liquor guy, his biggest vice was smoking—about a half-a-pack per day.

For George Herman Ruth, however, life in the *laissez-faire* twenties was lived in the fast lane.

The night before a big game in Washington, Senators star Goose Goslin invited Ruth for a night out on the town, intending to keep him up past sunrise. While Goslin limped back to his hotel, Ruth went to Walter Reed Army Hospital to sign baseballs for kids. That afternoon, he homered twice while Goslin went 0-for-5.

When a young fan asked Ruth whether he could hit .400 by concentrating on hits rather than homers, the slugger said, "*Four* hundred? Hell, I could hit *five* hundred!"

Always good for an off-handed remark, Ruth was the Yogi Berra of his day. After telling a writer he read books, the journalist asked what he thought of the Napoleonic Era. "I think it should have been scored a hit," Ruth blurted.

During Ruth's day, baseball consisted of two eight-team leagues that played 154-game seasons exclusively by daylight. He didn't have to worry about seeing the ball at night, the jet lag caused by air travel, an endless stream of hard-throwing relief pitchers, or instant exposure on electronic media. Radio was such a new medium that the outgoing Ruth once got stage fright during an interview.

For the first four years of his career, Aaron did not have to worry about cross-country plane trips either. But then the Dodgers and Giants left New York for California, where they began playing in 1958.

"One of the toughest things about playing today is the travel," he once said. "When you make that swing out to the West Coast to play the Dodgers, Giants, and Padres, your sleeping and eating habits get all messed up. Those early morning arrivals are a rat race. I notice that certain pitchers give me trouble out there, but I seem to be able to handle them back in our park."

While Ruth had the benefit of Lou Gehrig batting behind him for most of his career, Aaron had Eddie Mathews and, at various times, Joe Adcock, Joe Torre, Rico Carty, Orlando Cepeda, Earl Williams, and Dusty Baker. Aaron and Mathews not only hit a record 863 home runs as teammates, but connected in the same game 75 times, another mark.

"If the man hitting behind me has a good year," Aaron explained, "opposing pitchers can't pitch around me. They have to give me some pitches to hit. I'm as good as the fellow hitting behind me."

Aaron, a guess hitter who made a science of studying opposing pitchers, had a memory that could rival a contemporary computer. He also had the ability to wait until a pitch was almost past him before unleashing his quick, lightning-like wrists from an awkward, flat-footed stance that defied all hitting textbooks.

"He developed his own style as a young player and kept it throughout his career," said Mathews of his longtime teammate. "Young players shouldn't try to copy him. It would sound wrong to say the man destined to break Babe Ruth's career home run record had a fundamental flaw in his batting stance so let's just say Hank Aaron hit differently than anyone else."

Aaron swung a Louisville Slugger that measured 35 inches long from knob to handle but, unlike other stars, never visited the Hillerich & Bradsby bat factory in Louisville, Kentucky. He paid no heed to the trademark, which most hitters prefer on the topside because the bat is less likely to break if the ball hits a smooth surface. Aaron had a habit of twirling the bat in his hands until it felt comfortable, causing catcher John Roseboro to complain, "Your bat is facing the wrong way!" Cool as ever, Aaron said, "I didn't come up here to read."

Ruth's bat was a half-inch longer than Aaron's but a lot heavier—perhaps explaining why so many of his home runs had more mileage than his Roadster. Ruth was reputed to use a 54-ounce weapon, widely believed to be the heaviest in baseball history.

Neither man fanned as many as 100 times in a season, though such triple-digit frustration has long since become expected in today's game.

In contrast to Aaron, who was once so small that the Brooklyn Dodgers rejected him from their tryout camp, Ruth was built like a pot-bellied stove, with massive shoulders and forearms. In his prime, he was 6-foot-2 and 235 pounds—if the scales in the Yankee Stadium clubhouse were recording accurately.

Both players commanded the best salaries of their day, $80,000 for Ruth and $240,000 for Aaron some forty years later, but joined off-season barnstorming tours to increase their income.

When writers told Ruth he was making $5,000 more than Depression-era President Herbert Hoover, he reportedly said, "Yeah, but I had a better year than he did."

Flamboyant to a fault, Ruth even played the piano, a great device for making himself the center of attention at parties. Aaron preferred peace, quiet, and solitude, though the ability of a Black player to accompany white teammates to taverns after games was never easy.

Six years after he retired, Ruth's name was still so synonymous with the United States that Japanese troops goaded American GIs by shouting "To hell with Babe Ruth!"

Even after he died in 1948, the charismatic Ruth had a larger-than-life image not only in baseball, but the country as a whole. No one has been able to challenge it, even to this day.

"I don't want to make people forget Babe Ruth," Aaron said during the heat of his challenge. "I just want them to remember Henry Aaron."

Like Ruth, who aimed at short right-field dimensions in both the Polo Grounds and Yankee Stadium, Aaron benefitted from his surroundings—especially after the Braves moved from Milwaukee to Atlanta. The city's altitude, coupled with the stadium's 330-foot measurements down the lines, proved so conducive to Aaron's power that he deliberately became a pull hitter.

"I'm favored by a hitter's ballpark," Aaron admitted, "but they couldn't pitch around the Babe either."

There was no pressure on Ruth as he kept piling up home runs late in his career. His last one, against Guy Bush of the Pittsburgh Pirates, flew over the right-field roof at Forbes Park on May 25, 1935. Although it was No. 714, it had no significance at the time other than being the first ball to clear that roof.

Aaron's longest came on May 12, 1962, when he reached the center-field bleachers of the Polo Grounds with the bases loaded against Jay Hook, a mechanical engineer who could explain the dynamics of a curveball but couldn't throw one. It came one night after Lou Brock, then with the Cubs, also reached the distant seats.

Years later, when it became apparent that he could reach Ruth's record, Aaron faced the double whammy of pursuing the most revered record in sports and being a Black man chasing a white man's mark.

Both broke new ground: Ruth as the leader of the Live Ball Era that started in 1920, and Aaron as the symbol of success for Black America. Before Ruth, no American Leaguer had hit more than 16 home runs in a season. In 1920, he actually hit more home runs by himself than all seven teams in the AL.

Like Jackie Robinson before him, Aaron was a role model—as a player and a person—to legions of Black youngsters. During the final days of the 1973 season, then-fiancée Billye Williams said they often discussed Black issues and read books by and about Dr. Martin Luther King, Jr., the late civil rights leader.

Although Ruth never realized his post-career ambition of managing a major-league team, Aaron returned to Atlanta as player development director after Ted Turner purchased the team.

"I can't comment on what Ruth faced," Aaron said late in his career, "I don't really care what anyone says about times at bat. I've got 3,700 hits and Babe didn't get that."

A guess hitter, Aaron excelled at figuring out what a pitcher would throw. "When I'm hitting well," he once said, "I can tell what a pitch will be when it's halfway to home plate."

Ted Williams, baseball's best hitter between the peaks of Ruth and Aaron, agreed. "He knows more about the pitchers in the National League than anyone playing today," said Williams, a .344 lifetime hitter. "He waits for his pitch and makes them throw it."

Ruth had the same ability, according to shortstop-turned-manager Leo Durocher, a one-time Ruth roomate who became a Hall of Fame manager. "The Babe never made a mistake," he said. "He never threw to the wrong base and was a much better outfielder than you thought he was. He could run pretty well for a big man too. He could do a lot of things."

He could even hit for average, as his .342 lifetime mark suggests. But the overall league average of .282 during Ruth's peak fell to .252 during Aaron's, closing the 30-point differential between Ruth's career mark and the .310 mark Aaron had when his Braves tenure ended after the 1974 season.

Aaron and Ruth started and ended their careers in the same cities but with different teams in different leagues. Ruth came to the majors with the Boston Red Sox in 1914, had his biggest years with the Yankees, but finished in 1935 with the Boston Braves—the same franchise that was later based in Milwaukee and Atlanta. Aaron, though signed by the Boston Braves, never played there; he went from the 1954 Milwaukee Braves to the 1976 Milwaukee Brewers. Both spent most of their careers playing right field.

"I didn't always think 'home run' when I came to the plate," Aaron conceded after topping Ruth's record. "I was concentrating on getting a hit, trying to win the game. If a home run was needed, then I thought it was my duty to try and get it. First you play baseball, then you play to win, and then you go for home runs. The understanding of the fans is important."

The fans understood. After a year-long poll revealed at a New York news conference preceding the 1976 All-Star Game luncheon in Philadelphia, Aaron's 715th home run was voted Most Memorable Moment in baseball history, while Ruth was named the game's Most Memorable Personality. His daughter, Julia Ruth Stevens of Conway, New Hampshire, accepted the award for her late father.

CHAPTER 3

JACKIE'S HEIR

As a boy growing up in segregated Mobile, Alabama, Henry Aaron and his siblings hid under a bed while the Ku Klux Klan marched down the street in front of their house.

As a man pursuing the biggest record in professional sports, the sheets of ignorance remained—forcing him to find hotels and restaurants separate from those of his teammates.

All because he happened to be Black.

"I had many death threats," he said. "I couldn't even open letters for a long time because they had to be opened by the FBI or somebody else. I had to be escorted everywhere.

"Even though I did something great, nobody wanted to be a part of it. I was so isolated. I couldn't share it. For many years, even after Jackie Robinson, baseball was still so segregated. Baseball was meant for the lily-white."

Even the writers were worried; *Atlanta Journal* sports editor Lewis Grizzard wrote an Aaron obituary—just in case.

Just as he did early in his career, when segregation persisted long after Jim Crow laws were officially eliminated by the Supreme Court, Aaron had to live and eat separately from his teammates. As a kid, the issue was the malignant social climate of the country; as an adult, the issue was the repugnant attitude of anonymous bigots who hated the idea of a Black man replacing a white legend's name in the baseball record book.

As he approached the record in 1973, the avalanche of racially tinged hate mail grew. The Braves hired private security and a private secretary for Aaron, sneaking him into hotels under assumed names. At least when he went to Cleveland Browns football games, Aaron's disguise was only to ward off autograph seekers.

His family suffered as well. Only his wife and parents were present in Atlanta the night he hit his 715th home run, as his children were sequestered to their grandmother's house in Jacksonville out of concern for their safety.

"My kids had to live like they were in prison because of kidnap threats," he said, "and I had to live like a pig in a slaughterhouse. I had to duck. I had to go out the back door of ballparks. I had a police escort with me all the time and got threatening letters every day.

"All these things put a bad taste in my mouth and it wouldn't go away. They carved a piece of my heart away."

Bumper stickers that read AARON IS RUTHLESS appearing on Peachtree Street and other places in downtown Atlanta didn't help. "You have to be concerned," said Donald Davidson, the small but powerful traveling secretary of the team. "There are a lot of crazy people around. We've proven that in this country."

Worried about rumors of a red-coated assassin in the Atlanta ballpark, Aaron even told fellow outfielders Dusty Baker and Ralph Garr, two young Black stars, not to sit near him on the dugout bench.

He rarely talked about the torrent of hate mail, though he often threw such letters on the clubhouse floor, where teammates could see for themselves. He got so much mail—930,000 pieces, according to the US Postal Service—that he received a plaque for getting the most mail of any non-political figure in the country.

A kidnap threat was even directed at daughter Gaile, then a senior at Fisk University. But most of the messages Aaron received were positive and encouraging. The good far outweighed the bad.

"For every letter I get against setting the record, I get about four or five for it," said Aaron. "Nowadays I think most people want to see all records erased."

When Babe Ruth was piling up 714 lifetime home runs thirty years earlier, he did not have the pressure of pursuing anyone's record but his own. Nor did the white slugger face a deluge of derogatory messages from an army of anonymous detractors.

"I had a rough time with it," he said of chasing Ruth's record. "I didn't enjoy myself. It was hard for me to enjoy something that I think I worked very hard for. God gave me the ability to play baseball but people in this country chipped away at me. So it was tough. And all those things happened simply because I was a Black person.

"Babe Ruth never had to contend with anything like that when he was establishing his record."

As a boy, Aaron paid no attention to Ruth because baseball was segregated. That changed in 1947, when Robinson joined the Brooklyn Dodgers and integrated the game.

A year later, when Robinson came to Mobile, a fourteen-year-old Hank Aaron went to see him.

"When Jackie came to town in 1948, I skipped shop class to hear him speak at the auditorium on Davis Avenue," Aaron admitted. "That same day, I told my father I would be in the big leagues before Jackie retired."

Then he met Robinson, Roy Campanella, Don Newcombe, Junior Gilliam, Joe Black, and other Black stars of the Dodgers during a spring training barnstorming tour of the South that also involved the Milwaukee Braves.

With hotels and restaurants still off-limits, the Black players made separate arrangements—and spent lots of time playing cards and talking baseball.

"Those hotel rooms were my college," said Aaron, who learned as much about dealing with segregation as he did about baseball.

"In my first few years, I felt there was extra pressure on the Black ballplayers," he later revealed. "At that time there were so few Black ballplayers that in order for you to be on a ballclub, you couldn't be a fringe player. You had to be able to do twice as many things as the white players.

"Some of the white players sitting on the bench were making twice as much money as you were but you were out there playing every day.

"If there's a single reason why the Black players of the '50s and '60s were so much better than the white players in the National League, I believe it's because we had to be. And we knew we had to be."

Jackie Robinson, who won Rookie of the Year honors in 1947 and the National League's MVP trophy two years later, was the role model.

"Jackie had to be bigger than life," Aaron said of Robinson in a *Time* magazine article. "He had to be bigger than the Brooklyn teammates who got up a petition to keep him off the ballclub, bigger than the pitchers who threw at him, or the base-runners who dug their spikes into his shin, bigger than the bench jockeys who hollered for him to carry their bags and shine their shoes, bigger than the so-called fans who mocked him with mops on their heads and wrote him death threats."

Aaron couldn't say enough about Robinson, the first Black player enshrined in the National Baseball Hall of Fame.

"He was my idol. He gave every Black kid in America something to look forward to. He was intelligent, went about his business, and took all the pressure. People talk about the pressure on me but it's nothing compared to what Jackie went through."

Carrying on the legacy of Robinson, who retired after the 1956 season, was an enormous but worthwhile burden.

"I had a choice," Aaron said in his autobiography. "I could forget I was Black and just smile and go along with the program until my time was up or I could never forget I was Black. After hearing Jackie and the other Dodgers, there was only one way to make that choice."

Even if young Henry had wanted to forget his ethnicity, America would be quick to remind him.

When the Indianapolis Clowns, his Negro Leagues team, came to Washington for games, Aaron and his teammates were startled by the sound of dishes breaking in a restaurant kitchen. The staff was deliberately smashing the dishes the players had eaten off, rather than wash them.

Barnstorming through Dixie years later with an all-Black team organized by Willie Mays, Aaron and his teammates often had to scrounge for food or gas after night games. Light-skinned pitcher Sam Jones, who could pass for white, would show up at a segregated restaurant wearing a hat and pretending to be a deaf mute. He ordered food by pointing to his mouth and handing the cashier his order in writing.

By the time he reached the majors in 1954, Aaron had endured a difficult season in Jacksonville, where the Braves had a minor-league team in the all-white Sally League. Aaron, Felix Mantilla, and Horace Garner were sent there to change its complexion, but not even their teammates were keen on the concept.

After winning one game, Aaron and Mantilla were approached by a white fan outside the ballpark. "I just wanted to say that you niggers played a hell of a game," he said, thinking he was offering a compliment.

Aaron, still a teenager, roomed with Mantilla, a Puerto Rican infielder, and tried to protect him.

"Hank and I relied on each other," said Mantilla, who had a solid major-league career with the Braves, Red Sox, and other clubs. "We tried not to let the other one out of our sight. Hank tried to keep me away from the things that could have gotten me in trouble."

That meant, for example, steering clear of segregated movie theaters and restaurants. Aaron remembered seeing his father yield his place in line to a white man in a Mobile drugstore. Even his father's workplace at the Mobile docks had separate sections for whites and Blacks.

Like Robinson six years earlier, Aaron had to ignore racial epithets shouted from the stands—even in his home ballpark. Asked which of the other Sally League cities were more tolerable, he said, "None of them."

When he reached Milwaukee, manager Charlie Grimm immediately noted Aaron's slow but steady style, both at the plate and in the field. Without thinking, he called him "Stepin Fetchit" after a Black actor nicknamed "the laziest man in the world."

But Hank Aaron was anything but lazy; he was conserving his strength, picking his spots to uncork his quick wrists or dive after a ball.

Bill Bruton, a Black outfielder who reached the Braves one year earlier, took Aaron under his wing, just as Aaron would later do for Baker and Garr.

According to Claire Smith of ESPN, "He made sure the younger players knew they had a shoulder to lean on and that he would always have their backs. The support was important at a time when Black players were not celebrated but challenged. Aaron did not run from racism. He showed America, while playing in the heart of the South, how to be fearless, how to be a man."

Happy in Milwaukee, where he had a suburban home with Barbara, Aaron and his wife were more than a little agitated when the team announced its move to Atlanta. In fact, his first public reaction was that he didn't want to play there.

Henry was thinking of Lester Maddox, the restaurant owner who once barred Blacks with an ax handle, and other segregationists. And he remembered the bad old days in Mobile and Jacksonville. Barbara had endured hardships in the South, too, and was even more reluctant to go.

Speaking of the South, Aaron said, "I don't want to live there again. We can go anywhere in Milwaukee. I don't know what would happen in Atlanta.

"Returning to the South took some of the boy from Mobile out of me and replaced it with a man who was weary of the way things were. I was tired of being invisible."

In the long run, however, the move proved fortuitous for the future home run king. Like his hero Jackie Robinson, Aaron was integrating the South for the second time. He would be the first Black star on the first major-league team in the South.

Atlanta turned out to be a bastion of civility, even when the rest of Georgia was not. And the cozy dimensions and altitude of the new Atlanta Stadium enabled the Race with Ruth, though nobody voiced it at the time.

Dealing with segregated facilities wasn't over, however. Bradenton, where the Braves trained for years before moving to West Palm Beach, still had separate hotels, restaurants, rest rooms, and even water fountains. So did a few National League cities that bordered on the South.

In 1961, Aaron and several teammates convinced Braves general manager John McHale to have segregation eliminated at the Bradenton ballpark and to move the whole team to a hotel outside town that was willing to accept all of them.

"One time in Bradenton," said teammate Eddie Mathews, "Hank, Bob Buhl, and I were walking along the street, and I suggested we have a beer. Hank didn't like the idea and I immediately realized why. He thought he would be refused service because he's Black."

For Aaron, the elephant in the room was always his own race, which superseded the Race with Ruth. "I've often tried to imagine over the years how many home runs I would have hit if I didn't have all those other things happening," he mused, "but I was able to concentrate on what I needed to do at the plate and on the field.

"When I got into the batter's box, I never thought about anything but baseball. The good Lord took care of me in that regard. If it hadn't been for him, I don't know what I would have done."

Aaron, who sometimes slept in a storage room at the ballpark as he neared the record, said he sometimes feared for his life. When a firecracker went off by accident at Olympic Stadium in Montreal, he initially thought it was a gunshot.

Change came slowly.

Aaron lost a hero when President John F. Kennedy, for whom he had campaigned in Wisconsin, was assassinated in 1963. But his successor, Lyndon B. Johnson, signed a landmark civil rights bill in 1964, followed a year later by a voting rights law. Then came 1968, with the assassinations of Robert F. Kennedy and Dr. Martin Luther King Jr., a civil rights icon from Atlanta who had established a firm friendship with Aaron.

Six years later, when Aaron asked the Cincinnati Reds to devote a moment of silence to King's memory on the anniversary of his death, the team declined. Racism had again reared its ugly head.

Robinson was gone by then, passing away on October 24, 1972, leaving an enormous legacy that Major League Baseball remembers each year on April 15, when all teams wear his universally retired No. 42.

"I feel it is my responsibility to keep his dreams alive," Aaron said at the time. But racial tensions lingered in both baseball and the nation at large.

"I am so proud that I knew Jackie, that I hung around with him whenever I could, that I listened to his words, and followed his example as much as I could."

Racial considerations probably precluded Aaron from winning more than one MVP Award and certainly seemed present in voting for the Hall of Fame's Class of 1982, when the home run king was entirely omitted from the 10-name ballots of nine voters. He was also bypassed for managerial openings—as were other Black candidates before Frank Robinson finally landed one with the Cleveland Indians in 1975.

"I've been traveling for twenty years and I'm tired of it," Aaron said as his playing career came to a close, "and that's one of the reasons I don't wish to get into managing. But there are plenty of Black players who are well-qualified."

Al Campanis, vice president and general manager of the Los Angeles Dodgers, said on national television in 1987 that Blacks "lacked the basic necessities" to serve as managers or executives.

Shortly after the Campanis episode, Aaron and Jesse Jackson, the Chicago-based civil rights champion, met with baseball commissioner Peter Ueberroth to discuss the issue of pervasive racism in baseball.

"I have tried to be a home run hitter off the field, too," Aaron said. "I may not have hit the huge home runs that Jackie Robinson hit or that Martin Luther King and Jesse Jackson hit but at least I'm hitting line drives and maybe some of them will clear the fences."

Twelve years later, Braves closer John Rocker issued racist remarks in separate interviews with *Bill Mazeroski's Baseball Yearbook* and *Sports Illustrated*. "I have no place in my heart for people who feel that way," said Aaron, who received a public apology from the pitcher, whom the Braves traded to Cleveland after deciding he had a million-dollar arm and a ten-cent head.

That same year, Aaron became the first Black majority owner of a BMW franchise and pursued various venues for bringing more Black players into baseball.

The last major leaguer who actually played in the Negro Leagues, Aaron was also baseball's bridge from the Jackie Robinson Era.

"It bothers me that even though players today may have heard of Jackie Robinson, they don't know what he went through with the abuse, the death threats," Aaron told writer Ira Berkow. "Too many of the Black athletes today think the battle is won. It's not won. Not by a long shot."

In a 1993 interview with *Sport*, Aaron said, "I hate the way baseball has treated minorities. It has the worst record in sports."

Five years later, when owners made, for the first time by unanimous vote, one of their own the new commissioner of baseball, Aaron wondered aloud why they settled on Milwaukee Brewers owner Bud Selig. "There's no chance in hell I'll convince the owners I'm qualified to be Commissioner," he said. "Let's face it: I'm a Black man."

Although he eventually became a millionaire able to donate huge sums to scholarship funds and hospitals, he never forgot his roots.

"I believed there was a reason why I was chosen to break the record," he said years after it happened. "It was my task to carry on where Jackie Robinson left off."

Jacksonville Giant

When Hank Aaron was a 19-year-old player breaking the color line at Jacksonville in 1953, teammate Joe Andrews, a white first baseman, handled the racists in the stands and even ate with the Black players after bringing them food. "We couldn't talk back to the fans but Joe sure could and he damn sure did," Aaron wrote in his autobiography. Andrews, a bonus baby from Massachusetts, never made the majors. But he wore No. 44 with distinction in the minors.

Famous Guests

When he lived in Atlanta, Hank Aaron's dinner guests included civil rights icons Maynard Jackson, Andrew Young, and Dr. Martin Luther King, Jr.

CHAPTER 4
MARCH TO MILWAUKEE

Fifty bucks.

That's what prevented Hank Aaron and Willie Mays from winding up on the same team.

"I had the Giants contract in my hand," Aaron acknowledged years later," but the Braves offered $50 a month more. That's the only thing that kept Willie and me from being teammates."

The Giants were in such a hurry to sign him that they dashed off a telegram with the future slugger's name spelled "Arron." That didn't help their cause either.

"I thought my chances to make the Braves were better and that they were being more fair to me," Aaron recalled.

For a kid in the segregated Mobile, Alabama suburb of Toulminville, Boston's offer was big bucks—not to mention a big opportunity in a world that was finally opening doors that had not only been slammed shut, but also locked for nearly a century.

Already rejected by the Brooklyn Dodgers because scouts at their 1949 tryout camp thought the skinny fifteen-year-old was too small, Aaron had wanted to play baseball at an early age. But his father, a boilermaker's assistant on the city's docks who was mindful that the major leagues were segregated at the time (and had played semi-pro ball himself when there was no chance to advance), told him he couldn't.

Then he expressed interest in becoming an airline pilot. Again, his father turned thumbs down. "There are no Black airline pilots," he told his disappointed son.

The young Aaron skipped classes, spending time in pool halls and mastering eye-hand coordination by hitting bottlecaps with broomsticks. He once angered his mom by converting her favorite mop into a stickball bat.

Then Jackie Robinson happened. The same Brooklyn Dodgers who would later reject Aaron from their tryout camp shocked the segregated baseball world by signing Robinson and bringing him to the big leagues on April 15, 1947. Along with many others, Aaron was paying attention.

"I remember cutting a class in high school to hear Jackie speak at the baseball park in Mobile," Aaron said. "I was supposed to be in shop at the time but he was going to speak at 2:30 in the afternoon. He talked about baseball and what the future held for Black players in the major leagues. That gave me a little hope at that time. I went back and told my father and he said, 'If that is what you want to do, fine, be a baseball player.' He was a very sports-minded man himself and he helped me."

But Henry was only thirteen then and still growing. He could also play baseball—even though he developed an odd, cross-handed swing unlike any professional player before or since.

From 1950–1953, he made more moves than chess master Bobby Fischer.

The third of eight children (four boys) produced by Herbert and Estelle Aaron, he attended two schools—Central High for two years and then the Josephine Allen Institute—but was best known for playing football, using his speed and arm to become a fine halfback/end who received a football scholarship offer from Florida A&M. Neither high school had a baseball team, so the future home run king played softball instead during his days at Central. The team lost only three games in the two years Aaron was on the roster.

He was clearly bitten by the baseball bug—especially after Robinson broke the color line and opened the gates for Aaron and other talented Black players.

Henry started as a spring and summer softball player, then accepted a semi-pro contract that paid $3 a game from the Mobile Black Bears, who used him as a third baseman and outfielder in a league dominated by older players. After that team faced the Indianapolis Clowns in an exhibition game, the seventeen-year-old Aaron was offered $200 a month to join the barnstorming franchise.

Suddenly, a kid who had never been away from home was headed out into an unfamiliar world.

Henry Aaron, whose mother would not allow him to travel with the Black Bears, was becoming a man before he could vote, drink, or be drafted.

"I was in a new, lonesome world," he said later. "The travel was rough. Sometimes we'd play three games in a day, like two in Washington and one in Baltimore. We slept in hotels only on weekends and on the bus the rest of the time."

When he boarded the Louisville & Northern train to join the Clowns, the baggy pants Aaron was wearing—hand-me-downs from his older sister— had $2 in the pocket. He also had a couple of sandwiches prepared by his mom for the first road trip of his career.

"It was the first time in my life I had been around white people," Aaron wrote in *I Had a Hammer*. "I listened to those wheels carrying me farther away from home and tried to talk myself out of getting off at the next stop and going back.

"I've never stopped wondering if I did the right thing that day. I didn't know anything about making a living or taking care of myself or about the white world I'd have to face sooner or later.

"I didn't know what I wanted to be doing when I was forty or any of the other things I needed to know to make a decision that would affect me for the rest of my life—except for one. I knew I loved to play baseball and had the feeling I might be pretty good at it."

The white world was a vast unknown to the scared kid, who remembered hiding under his bed as the Ku Klux Klan marched down his street in Mobile. In his spare time, Aaron read comic books and sports magazines rather than play with friends. But team sports was different: it involved a group.

Ed Scott, the former Negro Leaguer who managed the Mobile Black Bears, recommended Aaron to Bunny Downs, business manager of the Indianapolis Clowns. The teenaged Aaron signed with the barnstorming team on November 20, 1951, and followed up by hitting .366 with five home runs, 41 hits, and nine stolen bases in 26 official games for the Negro American League team during a stay that lasted only three months. During his tenure, he battled racism, insecurity, and severe bouts of homesickness. On several occasions, brother Herbert Aaron actually had to talk young Henry into staying with the team.

In the meantime, Aaron's abilities had caught the eye of Boston Braves scout Dewey Griggs.

Griggs loved the young shortstop, but had to convince Braves ownership to pay Indianapolis $10,000 for his contract. He also had to convince Clowns owner Syd Pollack to accept that offer and Aaron to sign his first professional contract with a major-league organization, for $350 a month and a cardboard suitcase.

He did, on June 12, 1952—ending the quest of the New York Giants, who had already brought Mays to the majors. The Braves completed the deal with ten minutes to spare because farm director John Mullen had forgotten to send the confirmation telegram regarding the signing.

Aaron's goal was to reach the Boston Braves . . . but that never happened, as the troubled franchise shifted to Milwaukee during 1953 spring training. Aaron, meanwhile, was a unanimous choice for Northern League Rookie of the Year in 1952, his first season in organized ball. Though he played just 89 games, he hit .336 with 116 hits, 89 runs scored, zero home runs, and 61 runs batted in.

Billy Southworth, manager-turned-scout for the Boston Braves, went to Eau Claire for a first-hand look and was impressed by the team's new prospect. Correctly predicting the neophyte's potential, Southworth sent in a glowing scouting report of Aaron.

"He runs better than average so I would have to call him fast but not very fast," he wrote. "He is a line-drive hitter who has hit a couple of balls out of the park for home runs.

"He has good hands, also quick hands, gets balls away fast and accurately. His arm is strong.

"For a baby-faced kid of eighteen, his playing ability is outstanding. I will see the remaining games tonight but will send in this report now because regardless of what happens tonight, I will not change my mind in the least about this boy's ability."

Sent to Class A Jacksonville of the South Atlantic League by the newly named Milwaukee Braves in 1953, Aaron, roommate Felix Mantilla, and fellow Black prospect Horace Garner had the formidable task of integrating the all-white circuit, one of two still active at that time. Like Jackie Robinson, they had to overcome a barrage of racist taunts while producing against a better level of pitching.

Housed and fed separately from his teammates, Aaron feasted instead on opposing pitchers. Nurtured and instructed by Ben Geraghty, whom he always called his best manager, Henry led Jacksonville to the Sally League title with a .362 average, 338 total bases, 208 hits, 115 runs scored, 14 triples, and 22 home runs.

He missed a Triple Crown by a whisker when Tommy Giordano, later a long-time scout, hit two more home runs. Asked by Geraghty to give Aaron some pointers on playing defense, Giordano said, "Put him in the outfield. He's got a great arm."

As a hitter, his ability was obvious. Not so much as a fielder.

"He just stood up there flicking those wrists and simply overpowered the opposition," remembered Geraghty, whose team brought Jacksonville its first flag in forty-one years.

The forty-one-year-old manager, a wartime utility infielder for the Boston Braves, endeared himself to his three Black players by visiting with them on the road—giving them a chance to talk baseball and relieve some of the pressure from the hostile environment. Aaron was a special project for Geraghty, who encouraged him to wait longer, recognize the pitch, and hit it hard.

The kid's temperament helped. "The most relaxed kid I ever saw," Geraghty said of Aaron in a 1957 *Sports Illustrated* article. "From the time we got on the bus until we got to the next town, Hank was asleep. Nothing ever bothered him."

Though wide awake on the field, Aaron finished his Sally League sojourn with 36 errors—a lot for a second baseman— against eight for Giordano. He also succeeded in turning a deaf ear to the ballpark bigots.

"Henry never spoke about it and never made any complaints," his father said years after the fact. "I believe if you start to worry about complaints, it's going to take a lot from you."

Aaron later revealed that there wasn't a safe haven in the circuit. "They were all bad," he said, referring to Montgomery, Macon, Savannah, and several South Carolina sites.

"Baseball is hard enough when everyone is rooting for you," said Jim Frey, a Jacksonville teammate who later managed in the majors. "It was just terrible what he was subjected to."

Taking a page from the Robinson playbook, Aaron let his bat speak on his behalf. After running away with the league's MVP honors, Aaron not only found success on the diamond that year but also off the field. He married Barbara Lucas on October 6, 1953. They didn't have much of a honeymoon, however, as the Braves sent young Henry to the Puerto Rican Winter League.

There, under Caguas manager Mickey Owen, the iron-handed second baseman not only showed he could hit to all fields but also make a smooth transition to the outfield, showing an aptitude for running, catching, and throwing that would later earn him three Gold Gloves. Owen also taught Aaron how to distribute his weight and hold his hands properly while batting. But he left the youngster's self-taught batting stance—the by-product of a schoolboy ankle injury—alone.

"I've seen a kid who could turn out to be a better ballplayer than Willie Mays," gushed Giants scout Tom Sheehan, who later managed that team in San Francisco. "His name is Henry Aaron."

The Braves, worried that Aaron might follow Mays into the military, somehow convinced Aaron's draft board to leave him alone, contending that he was going to integrate the Southern Association with the Atlanta Crackers the following season.

As it turned out, Milwaukee was the only place Aaron was going. Manager Charlie Grimm had read the glowing scouting reports, but seeing was believing. Hank Aaron hardly needed any more seasoning—he was already a well-done product, looking only for a place to play.

That wasn't easy with the Braves, a team packed better than Dolly Parton.

He reached the majors at age twenty in 1954 after veteran outfielder Bobby Thomson—yes, *that* Bobby Thomson—broke his leg sliding during spring training. It happened in the eighth inning of his first exhibition game with the team. That was all manager Charlie Grimm needed to find a spot in the lineup for Aaron.

"I just felt bad for Bobby," Aaron said. "It didn't occur to me at the time that it would be me who would replace him. A lot of fellows had good seasons in Triple-A and I had played only two years."

Given Thomson's spot in left field, Aaron made the most of his opportunity. In his first exhibition game, he hit a long home run—a portent of things to come, though nobody knew it at the time.

"Some of the fellows were a little skeptical when the Braves' front office told us this young kid, Henry Aaron, would be in spring training with us," Thomson remembered. "Everybody said he was bound to be a great one, but nobody gave him much thought. He'd hit well in the minors, but we figured he'd be like so many other rookies before him—come to camp with a reputation, really see the curveball for the first time, and bomb out."

Ty Cobb and Rogers Hornsby, owners of the top two batting averages in baseball history, raved about the rookie. The former called him "one of the best young players he has seen in years," according to the *Los Angeles Times*.

Hornsby, a former manager who became a batting coach for several clubs, was even more effusive in his praise. "Aaron can become an even better hitter than he is—maybe even a .400 hitter—with enough desire," the Rajah said. "In addition to all the natural ability in the world, it takes heart, guts, and desire. I became a better hitter because I wanted to badly enough.

"He has the kind of wrists and whip swing that enable him to wait until the last split second and to get a piece of the ball even on pitches that have fooled him.

"Somebody said Aaron has great hips. Hips? Hell, you don't hit a baseball with your rear end. What Aaron has is a smooth pivot that gives him power. He has made use of what the good Lord gave him—the eyes, arms, legs, and coordination of a natural hitter.

"If he pays attention to the strike zone it doesn't make any difference who the pitcher is, what arm he throws with, or what the pitch is. If Aaron makes them put the ball in there, he can hit it.

"He hits with power to all fields and that's the test of a hitter—hitting the ball where it's pitched. That takes timing."

The young Aaron also had good timing—not to mention good instincts—in the outfield. "When he first came up," said Bill Bruton, a rookie outfielder himself a year earlier, "I used to hold my breath when a fly ball was hit to him. Then I realized that he always ambled after a ball like that but always got to it. After a while, I stopped worrying."

By the time the season started, Aaron had befriended Bruton, a fleet Black center fielder who had reached the majors at age twenty-seven in 1953 and promptly led the National League with 26 stolen bases. "He was like a big brother and father to me, all at the same time," Aaron acknowledged. "He was a bit older than I was and a very intelligent player. I talked to him quite a lot and got to know his wife and family. If it weren't for Bill Bruton, I don't know if I would have made it in those early years."

While Bruton embraced Aaron's arrival, the shy rookie was not so comfortable around Eddie Mathews. "It was natural for me to be very conscious of Eddie, maybe even a little awed by him," Aaron admitted. "After all, he was a big star, the home run champion of the National League, and I was only a rookie. Chances are I didn't even introduce myself to him but just looked at him in the clubhouse and in the field."

For Aaron, those early years still included hotel and restaurant discrimination in places like Cincinnati and St. Louis, but he admitted playing in the big leagues was easier than getting there. He relished the fan enthusiasm for the 1954 Braves, who drew a league-record 2,133,388, but also appreciated his own anonymity, intimating he could walk down the streets of Milwaukee without being noticed.

One man who did notice him was Lou Perini, then the owner of the Braves. He asked about Aaron's family and told him about his own, including a wife and seven children. That gave the rookie growing confidence in both his persona and his baseball skills.

His teammates had to overcome their initial doubts about Aaron. Joe Adcock wondered if he would hit, while Eddie Mathews and Warren Spahn initially reserved judgement. It didn't take long, however, before Spahn silenced the skeptics in the clubhouse. "Let the Dodgers find his blind spot," said the star southpaw, "and that's if he has one."

Though the wiry Aaron didn't look anything like the typical muscular slugger, he hit his first home run against aging veteran Vic Raschi of the St. Louis Cardinals, then added a dozen more before breaking his own leg in an awkward September slide. The only major injury of his 23-year career, it probably cost him the 1954 Rookie of the Year Award.

But Aaron had made a good first impression—and set some personal goals for himself. "I wanted to play ball for 20 years and be successful at playing it," he revealed years later. "I said I would like to accomplish certain things—and set my goal kind of high.

"I wanted to get 3,000 base-hits. I wasn't thinking in terms of 700 home runs but maybe reaching 400. I felt if I could reach those goals, I could be fairly successful in baseball."

As a rookie, he had 131 hits in 122 games. But he was a work in progress.

"The Sally League was a fastball league," he recalled, "but in the majors, I had to learn to hit the off-speed stuff. I learned to hit the change-up of Carl Erskine of the Brooklyn Dodgers. I just said to myself I was going to wait on the pitch and be patient."

Raschi, who yielded both his first hit and his first homer, quickly developed respect for his rival. "Nobody on our team knew anything about Aaron except Eddie Stanky, our manager," he said. "He knew Henry was a potentially fine player and he talked about everything except the way he parted his hair. He could run, field, throw, and of course hit. He had such great wrists, like Ernie Banks, that it was hard to fool him."

Aaron's season came to a screeching halt on September 5, when the Braves were five games behind the Giants and still mindful of making a late run for the flag. After taking an 11–8 verdict in the first game of a double-header against Cincinnati, Aaron hit a long drive that landed in center field, looking to everyone in the ballpark like a certain triple—and his fifth hit of the day.

But the fates had other plans. Aaron broke his ankle sliding into third and was lost for the season.

Then Joe Adcock suffered a broken wrist when hit by a Don Newcombe pitch.

"You'll never guess who came in to run for me," Aaron said. "Bobby Thomson himself. Bobby begins the season in the hospital, I take his job, and I end the season in the hospital and he gets his job back. By that time, though, I knew something I didn't know when Bobby went to the hospital: I knew I could play in the big leagues."

With two sluggers gone, so were the team's pennant chances. The Braves wound up finishing third, eight games behind the Giants and three behind the Dodgers, with an 89–65 record.

It was in Milwaukee that Aaron met Donald Davidson, the diminutive but often demonstrative executive whose malaprops and propensity for cursing made him a legend throughout the National League. It was Davidson, who barely reached 48 inches in height, who handed Hank Aaron his first jersey—No. 5—but begrudgingly switched it to No. 44 a year later.

"You're so skinny," he told Aaron, "that I don't know how a little bastard like you could carry two numbers around."

Davidson told Aaron that single digits adorned the uniforms of such greats of the game as Babe Ruth (3), Lou Gehrig (4), Joe DiMaggio (5), Stan Musial (6), and Ted Williams (9). But the rookie couldn't be dissuaded.

"After I assigned him No. 44," said Davidson of Aaron, "he hit 44 home runs four times in his career. So I regret I did not give him No. 70."

Davidson also made another history-making decision: he started calling the kid "Hank" instead of his preferred "Henry." The nickname took.

After suffering through the purgatory of playing in the Deep South when statehouses still flew the Stars & Bars, Aaron enjoyed the serenity of Wisconsin.

"I never had anything but good feelings for the people of Milwaukee," he said. "It's a wonderful town and the people were very kind to me. I always lived in integrated neighborhoods, without problems."

Although the winds and chilly temperatures at Milwaukee County Stadium were hardly conducive to home run production, Henry Aaron found the range, albeit in his fourth season.

That happened in 1957, the first year since 1948 that the National League pennant went to a team that did not play in New York.

CHAPTER 5
WINNING A RING

The Milwaukee Braves were the only team in baseball history to never have a losing season.

Overshadowed by the Red Sox in Boston, the Braves arrived in Milwaukee with high expectations heading into spring training in 1953. A mix of veterans and rising young stars, their future got an enormous boost from the energy and enthusiasm of their new fan base— plus the energy and enthusiasm of their first home-grown fan favorite, Henry Louis Aaron.

Although Aaron was a minor-league infielder in 1953 while the Braves were still getting their feet wet in Wisconsin, he found his way to the front lines a year later.

In a real rags-to-riches story, the Braves rebounded from a 64–89 final season in Boston to a 92–62 Milwaukee debut that left them second in the standings, 13 games behind the powerful Brooklyn Dodgers, but first in attendance, with a new National League record (1.82 million) after drawing only 282,000 to Braves Field the season before.

Suddenly, the erstwhile ragamuffins had blossomed into bona fide contenders. After adding Aaron as the result of a spring training mishap that sidelined newly acquired Bobby Thomson, the Braves got 40 home runs from Eddie Mathews, a four-homer game from Joe Adcock, and 21 wins from Warren Spahn en route to a solid third-place showing, eight games behind the New York Giants and three behind second-place Brooklyn with an 89–65 mark.

Speaking of Aaron, Mathews said, "We knew he had a tremendous amount of talent, we knew he could play, we knew he could hit, but that's about all we knew."

A year later, with Aaron healed from his own sliding fracture, the Braves bounced back to a second-place finish, closing the season at 85–69, though 13.5 games behind the Dodgers. In his second season, the wiry Aaron became a sudden slugger—more than doubling his rookie year production, from 13 homers to 27—while leading the National League with 37 doubles to go along with a .314 batting average.

It was in 1956, however, that the Braves finally showed they were more than also-rans. Sluggish at the start with a 24–22 mark on June 16, the Braves dumped manager Charlie Grimm for Fred Haney, who coaxed his charges to an immediate 11-game winning streak and a 68–40 record. But it was one game too short, even though the Braves had taken a one-game lead into the final weekend.

The Braves lost two of three in St. Louis to close out the season, finishing 14–13 in September, while the Dodgers swept Pittsburgh.

Aaron couldn't be blamed: En route to his first batting title (.328), also led the league in doubles (34), and total bases (340), while leading all of baseball in hits (200). Mathews and Adcock also added considerable power, while Warren Spahn, Lew Burdette, and Bob Buhl were just as potent as pitchers, with

Buhl posting an 8–1 record against Brooklyn alone (he won 10 more against the other six teams in the league).

The Braves could smell the festive meal, but the taste would have to wait another year.

In 1957, when the world was otherwise preoccupied with Elvis Presley, Sputnik, and the never-ending push to de-segregate Southern schools, the Milwaukee Braves enjoyed their best year to date.

It was also the only year that Hank Aaron either earned a World Series ring, symbolic of team excellence, or an MVP trophy, awarded by vote of the baseball writers. He won both that fall.

Aaron's statistics spoke for themselves: 44 home runs, a career-peak 132 RBIs, 118 runs scored, and 369 total bases—all league highs (with him leading all of baseball in home runs and RBIs). His batting average was a cool .322, though Aaron claimed his average—down six points from the previous year—would have been better if he hadn't stepped on a bottle thrown onto the field. Only Musial and Mays, with better batting averages, deprived him of a Triple Crown.

The 6-foot, 180-pound right-handed hitter didn't have the size of other sluggers but considered himself an RBI man who would be cheated if he didn't bat third or fourth.

Haney eventually concurred, dropping Aaron from second to fourth on May 25, but the switch proved no instant panacea. Aaron went 0-for-4 in his first game as cleanup man as Dick Drott of the Cubs fanned 15 Braves, helping Chicago to sweep a doubleheader.

Such off-days were few and far between for Aaron, a rare slugger who also made good contact. En route to a .600 slugging percentage in 1957, he fanned only 58 times.

Eddie Mathews, the left-handed slugger who often batted behind Aaron, collected his 200th home run on June 12, eventually finishing second on the team in hits (167), runs (109), total bases (309), RBIs (94), and home runs (32).

The Braves overcame injuries to powerful first baseman Joe Adcock, who played in 65 games before he was lost with a fractured fibula, and leadoff man Bill Bruton, who got into 79 contests before hurting his knee in a July 11 collision with Felix Mantilla and missing the rest of the season. Even Mantilla, a jack-of-all-trades, missed a month after the mishap.

Frank Torre, whose brother Joe would later win a batting title and MVP Award in the majors, replaced Adcock, improving the defense but not the offense, while fellow veteran Andy Pafko and youngsters Wes Covington and Bob "Hurricane" Hazle bolstered the outfield. But it was Aaron's willingness to shift to Bruton's vacated station in center that allowed Haney to rebuild the corners around him. He had never played the position before.

Covington contributed 21 homers in 96 games, while Hazle picked up his nickname—based on a devastating hurricane of the previous fall—with a .403 average, seven homers, and 27 RBIs in 41 games after arriving from Double-A Wichita.

The Braves probably saved their season with a deadline day trade June 15 that sent Bobby Thomson, Danny O'Connell, and Ray Crone to the New York Giants for second baseman Red Schoendienst. Thomson, whose ninth-inning home run ended the 1951 National League playoffs, was returning to familiar turf, but neither he nor O'Connell was hitting at the time the deal was made. Their averages were .236 and .235, respectively.

When Bruton was hurt, Haney had to improvise. He had the perfect replacement for the top of the lineup in Schoendienst, who had been the leadoff man for the 1946 Cardinals team that won the World Series. The spray-hitting second baseman batted .309 in 93 games for the Braves, supplied stalwart leadership, and wound up third in MVP voting, trailing only Aaron and St. Louis superstar Stan Musial.

"Without Red Schoendienst, we don't win," Aaron said afterward.

Aaron hit 11 home runs in June, the most prolific one-month power production of his career, and sparked talk about Babe Ruth for the first time.

Not that he might reach 714 in his career—no one was looking that far ahead—but that he might break the single-season record. With 27 home runs in the first 76 games, about half the season, his pace matched Ruth's 60-homer onslaught from 1927.

"With a natural hitter like Hank Aaron, anything is possible," Bill Bruton offered. "It's about time somebody started comparing Henry's homer record with Babe Ruth's."

For reasons unknown, Aaron had turned into a sudden slugger—after failing to reach 30 home runs in any of his first three seasons.

"I think Henry made up his mind he was going to hit more home runs," said catcher Del Crandall, one of six Braves who went to the All-Star Game in 1957. "I have no idea where he projected himself as far as how many home runs he was going to hit. But I think he decided he was going to be a home run hitter.

"To me, Henry Aaron was the best hitter I ever saw. He could have been a .350, .360 hitter, whatever he wanted to do."

In late June and early July, he had seven homers in eight days. By All-Star time, his .347 average was tops in the National League but not enough to keep the Braves in first place, which St. Louis held by 2.5 games.

Six Braves went to the Midsummer Classic after Baseball Commissioner Ford Frick placed Aaron and Willie Mays into the opening lineup as replacements for Wally Post and Gus Bell, two of the seven Cincinnati starters chosen by overzealous fans in a notorious ballot-stuffing scheme. The other Braves who went to St. Louis for the game were infielders Eddie Mathews, Johnny Logan, and Red Schoendienst, along with pitchers Warren Spahn and Lew Burdette.

When Aaron smacked his 29th home run on July 16, he began to look like the front-runner for MVP honors. The very next day, however, he tripped over a drainage board deep in the Shibe Park outfield while pursuing a two-run double by Willie "Pudding Head" Jones. His ankle swelled and cost him a week on the bench—while Andy Pafko, Johnny DeMerit, and even Red Schoendienst took turns trying to fill the gaping void in center field. Even Del Crandall, no paragon of speed, got to sow his oats in right field.

Haney, who had played for Ty Cobb before managing moribund ballclubs with the Pittsburgh Pirates and St. Louis Browns, wasn't about to blow his best shot at the World Series. He mixed and matched like a magician, even using journeyman Nippy Jones, who had been out of the majors since 1952.

And he convinced Mathews to work harder on both his defense at third base and his at-bats against left-handed pitchers.

The Braves clinched the pennant on September 23 when Aaron delivered a two-run home run in the 11th inning of a home game against the Cardinals. A rookie right-hander recalled a month before, Muffett had not yielded a home run in 44 innings before that moment in time.

Aaron, who had two singles, a walk, and a groundout during a tight 2–2 game that night, wasted little time, turning a hard curveball into a rocket that barely cleared Wally Moon's glove before landing in the thicket of pine trees dubbed "Perini's Forest" after Braves owner Lou Perini.

Although the outfielder had hit 42 previous home runs that season, that one had special meaning because it brought back memories of Bobby Thomson, whose "Shot Heard 'Round the World" home run for the New York Giants, on October 3, 1951, not only won a pennant but was heard on the radio by then seventeen-year-old Henry Aaron. The future home run king promised himself then and there that he would like nothing better than experiencing the euphoria of Thomson as he trotted around the bases.

"I had always dreamed of having a moment like Bobby Thomson had," Aaron said amid the clubhouse celebration afterward, "and that was it."

The next day, Aaron homered again, picking on a pitch from Sam "Toothpick" Jones with the bases loaded. That first-inning blast was his last home run of the year but one of the best, since it gave Aaron league leadership in home runs and was also the first of four times in which he would match his uniform number.

As a confident defense attorney might say, "The defense rests, your honor."

Playing in 151 games, Aaron led the league with 118 runs scored, 132 RBIs, 369 total bases, and 44 home runs (the last three leading all of baseball).

After a grueling pennant race that involved five teams, the Milwaukee Braves wrapped up their first pennant with a 95–59 record that left them eight games ahead of the runner-up St. Louis Cardinals. The Dodgers, in their final Brooklyn season but first since Jackie Robinson retired, were third, 11 games out, while the Cincinnati Reds finished fourth at 80–74, rounding out what was then called the first division.

The Braves, who were based in Boston when they won previous pennants in 1914 and 1948, had Milwaukee records for wins, winning percentage (.617), and attendance (2,220,000). Their 50 victories on the road also led the league.

In 1957, the best teams from each eight-team league went directly into the World Series without passing GO or collecting $200. Without an endless maze of playoffs, nothing could compromise the integrity of the final round.

Before the World Series began, Yankees icon Mickey Mantle lit a fire under the Braves by referring to Milwaukee as "Bushville," a derisive term for anything Midwestern.

By the time the World Series started in Yankee Stadium on October 2, the Braves were more than ready.

Though ready for a fight, and hoping to put Mantle's foot in his mouth, the Braves lost the opener, 3–1, in front of 69,476 fans in the Bronx. They got even the next day, however, with a 4–2 victory—marred only when supporters of Cuban revolutionary Fidel Castro littered the field with leaflets urging the overthrow of dictator Fulgencio Batista.

After losing a 12–3 rout in Milwaukee County Stadium for Game 3, the home team evened the best-of-seven series again with a 10-inning, 7–5 victory the following day.

Nippy Jones was the unexpected hero when, in the 10th inning, he proved he had been hit by a Tommy Bryne pitch when he showed plate umpire Augie Donatelli that the white ball had a fresh smudge of black shoe polish. Jones had no hits and no runs scored in three plate appearances, but that one hit-by-pitch made him a baseball legend.

After Bob Grim replaced Byrne, Felix Mantilla—running for Jones—moved to second on a bunt by Red Schoendienst and scored on a game-tying double by Johnny Logan. Then Eddie Mathews hit a two-run homer to break the 5–5 tie. Jones never batted in a major-league game again.

With the Series tied at two games apiece, Lew Burdette—winner of Game 2—went all the way in a 1–0 win that put the Braves within one win of a world championship over the heavily favored Yankees.

Back in New York, the Yankees rebounded for a 3–2 triumph in the sixth game before Burdette returned to the mound on short rest when Warren Spahn came down with the flu. With the Series on the line, he responded by pitching a 5–0 complete-game shutout in the Bronx on October 10 to wrap up the World Series and capture MVP honors (that could have gone to Aaron, whose .393 average, three home runs, and seven runs batted in led both teams).

"The Yankees came back to tie us after every home run I hit," Aaron said several years into his retirement, "so I can't rate any of them on my [favorites] list since none of them won a ball game."

Although the Braves would win another pennant in 1958 and finish in a first-place tie with the Dodgers a year later, Hank Aaron would never win another World Series ring.

Nor would he win another MVP trophy. Before the city of Milwaukee had even stopped celebrating its only world championship, Henry Louis Aaron was named National League MVP in a photo finish over seven-time batting champion Stan Musial. His margin of victory was just nine votes.

The coveted Player of the Year Award presented by *The Sporting News*, which could have also gone to Aaron, instead went to Ted Williams, who batted .388 for the Boston Red Sox at the advanced athletic age of thirty-nine.

Teammate Warren Spahn also went home for the winter with an extra prize when he became the first left-handed pitcher to win the Cy Young Award, then given to one pitcher per year. He went 21–11 with a 2.69 ERA, and worked 271 innings, including four relief outings that would have produced three saves under rules adopted later. Although he would win 20 games in 13 different seasons, throw two no-hitters, and finish his career with 363 wins—the most for any left-handed pitcher—the future Hall of Famer won the prestigious award only once.

After the season, the baseball map underwent a significant change when both the Dodgers and Giants announced they were leaving New York for sunny California.

Nine years later, the Braves would also relocate—for the second time—and change the fortunes of Hank Aaron forever.

CHAPTER 6

HEADING SOUTH

The Milwaukee Braves came *thisclose* to establishing a baseball dynasty during the late 1950s.

With Jackie Robinson retired and both the Dodgers and Giants pulling up stakes in New York, the Braves finished one game out in 1956, enjoyed a world championship season in 1957, won a pennant in 1958, and wound up in a first-place tie (and unscheduled best-of-three playoff) in 1959.

Then a slow fall began: second in 1960, fourth in 1961, fifth in 1962, and sixth in 1963 before two more sixth-place seasons.

With age overtaking some of the team's top stars, management traded such old heroes as Joe Adcock, Johnny Logan, Bill Bruton, Lew Burdette, and Bob Buhl—but foolishly sent away top pitching prospects Joey Jay and Juan Pizarro as well.

Milwaukee made a great trade, landing the original Frank Thomas for Mel Roach on May 9, 1961, but then sending Thomas to the expansion New York Mets for Gus Bell and $125,000 that November. The Braves also sent still-productive closer Don McMahon to the Houston Colts, the other NL expansion team. Both players could have helped the Braves in 1962 and beyond.

Nobody even considered unloading Hank Aaron but even he had to wonder what was happening all around him. One thing that was happening was fan disinterest.

The enthusiasm that greeted the former Boston Braves when they came to Milwaukee in 1953 was long gone, especially after the team imposed restrictions on bringing outside food and beverages into the ballpark. In a city known for its beer and breweries, that was as unthinkable as trading Aaron in his prime.

Nobody could prevent the bleeding.

The Braves had their last hurrah in 1958, when they reached the World Series for the second straight year. They even won three of the first four World Series games against the Yankees.

Warren Spahn won two games, including a Game 4 shutout, but lost Game 6, 4–3, in 10 innings, and Burdette wasn't as bulletproof as he had been a year earlier. When Aaron went homerless despite a .333 average, Milwaukee's fate was sealed.

Chances of another pennant suffered a major setback the following spring when Red Schoendienst, the aging but productive second baseman, came down with tuberculosis. He missed almost the whole season, with Haney trying to fill the void with a cast of characters that included Chuck Cottier, Felix Mantilla, Johnny O'Brien, Mel Roach, and Casey Wise. Roach hit .097—a great earned run average but terrible batting average—and none of the others did much better.

Nobody was hitting on May 26, a foggy night in Milwaukee. Pittsburgh pitcher Harvey Haddix, a little left-hander known as "The Kitten," threw 12 perfect innings, keeping the Braves at bay, while Lew Burdette matched him zero-by-zero.

Burdette, a fidgety right-hander often accused of throwing a spitball, needed no help from Mother Nature on that soggy night. But he got some from the Pirates in the bottom of the 13th.

Felix Mantilla was safe on a throwing error by third baseman Don Hoak, who had trouble gripping the slippery ball. After Eddie Mathews bunted him to second, Aaron was purposely passed, putting runners on first and second with one out.

Then Joe Adcock hit the ball over the fence, ostensibly ending the game with a 3–0 score. But Aaron, in the excitement of the moment, advanced only to second, then darted directly to the dugout when he saw the ball clear the wall. Adcock, with his head down in a home run trot, was out the minute he passed the spot Aaron had vacated. After a few days of wrangling, Adcock was given a double, Mantilla's run was the only one that counted, and 1–0 was the final score.

Aaron would not make such a mistake again. In fact, he was actually in the middle of a career-best year. Over .400 early, he finished at .355 while leading the league with 223 hits, 400 total bases, and a slugging percentage of .636.

He also hit three home runs in a game for the only time in his career—at San Francisco's Seals Stadium, temporary home of the relocated Giants, on June 21. His victims were former teammate Johnny Antonelli, a lefty, and righthanders Gordon Jones and Stu Miller.

Power partner Eddie Mathews hit 46 home runs, most in the league, because statistics from unscheduled pennant playoffs counted. Mathews, missing his career peak by one, broke a tie with eventual MVP Ernie Banks by connecting in the first game of the best-of-three playoffs.

The Dodgers won anyway, 3–2 and 6–5, when Haney made inexplicable decisions to start Carlton Willey (5–9, 4.15 during the season) in the opener and lift Lew Burdette in the ninth inning of Game 2 with a three-run lead. After a parade of relievers frittered it away, a throwing error by substitute shortstop Felix Mantilla—in for the injured Johnny Logan—ended the game in the 12th inning.

Haney never managed again, though his record with the Braves suggests he did a better job than any of his three successors, Charlie Dressen, Birdie Tebbetts, or Bobby Bragan.

The man in the manager's chair made no difference to Aaron. The first unanimous choice in an NL All-Star lineup then chosen by players, coaches, and managers, he hit his 200th home run against Ronnie Kline of the Cardinals on July 3, 1960, and a titanic clout into the distant bleachers of the Polo Grounds with the bases loaded against Jay Hook of the New York Mets two years later, on June 18, 1962. On July 12, he and brother Tommie, a 1962 rookie who was also his roommate, homered in the same game for the first time.

Always compared with Willie Mays, Aaron even combined with teammates Joe Adcock, Frank Thomas, and Mathews to become the first quartet of players to hit consecutive home runs in a game.

"Mays was at the top of his game when I broke into baseball," Aaron said. "From the very beginning, he was the guy I was measured against. It went on for as long as we played in the same league—20 years and then some."

Comparing the flamboyant Mays, who loved the bright lights of New York, with the soft-spoken Aaron, based in Middle America, was a non-starter even though they played the same position and parlayed power, speed, and defense into the pinnacle of baseball stardom. It was like comparing the guy who waves the flag with the guy who carries it over the finish line.

Henry always seemed to be a step ahead of Willie.

In 1963, Aaron made a serious bid to become the first National Leaguer with a Triple Crown since Joe Medwick in 1937 (Mays never won one either). He not only produced the lone 30/30 season of his career but led the league in home runs (44), runs (121), runs batted in (130), hits (201), and total bases. His final average was .319.

The Sporting News named Aaron Player of the Year for the second time, but the MVP trophy went to Sandy Koufax of the World Champion Los Angeles Dodgers.

Unfortunately for the Braves, most of Aaron's teammates weren't hitting their weight. The 1962 team posted its worst batting average since the team played in Boston and denied Spahn his seventh straight 20-win season despite a league-best 22 complete games and 3.04 ERA. Milwaukee finished fifth, Tebbetts lost his job, and even the owner had seen enough.

The Perini Corporation sold the club to the LaSalle Corporation, a Chicago-based syndicate, in November and rumors of relocation began almost immediately.

With attendance of less than a million for three straight seasons, National League owners gave the Braves permission to move to Atlanta for 1965. The decision was delayed for a year in court, making the Milwaukee Braves lame ducks only eight years after they were on top of the baseball world.

Aaron, meanwhile, did not want to turn into a sitting duck. With bitter memories of the rampant racism that extended from his boyhood to the minors and beyond, he was adamant about not returning to the South. Teammate Lee Maye, another Black outfielder from Alabama, publicly agreed but was then traded to Houston for Ken Johnson and Jim Beauchamp.

"I lived in the South and don't want to live there again," Aaron said as rumors morphed into facts. "This is my home. I've lived here since I was a nineteen-year-old kid. We can go anywhere in Milwaukee, but I don't know what would happen in Atlanta."

Barbara Aaron didn't know either. She was not only reluctant to sell her home in Milwaukee but also to take her four children out of integrated public schools in the city.

The one-year delay in the franchise transfer gave the Aarons considerable time for soul-searching. Reluctantly, they agreed.

"Milwaukee was home to me," Aaron lamented. "I came up as a kid there and in the twelve years I was there, they never booed me. I always felt I was part of Milwaukee."

Atlanta city fathers, headed by Mayor Ivan Allen, worked feverishly to recast the city's image, using their new, 50,000-seat stadium as the glittering cornerstone. They were determined that the capital of Georgia was going to be progressive even if the rest of the state wasn't.

They hosted Aaron and Mathews on a city tour in January 1965, six weeks before the start of spring training, and took them both to the ballpark and to upscale neighborhoods. Aaron bought a house in southeast Atlanta and moved in the following summer.

On the eve of the opener, the city held a parade "right down Peachtree," as broadcaster Ernie Johnson often said in describing pitches. The event included Playboy bunnies, Busch Clydesdales, and a curvaceous beauty purporting to be the Posture Queen of the Georgia Chiropractic Association.

Atlanta officials were clearly posturing. Uniformed players rode down the main drag in convertibles as ticker tape fell all around them, clowns cavorted, and bands blared.

Seeing Atlanta Fulton County Stadium for the first time eased Aaron's angst.

The cozy dimensions, combined with the city's high humidity and deceptively high altitude (then highest in baseball at that time), opened the slugger's eyes. "The ball carried so well that Hank changed his hitting style," said Mathews, whose first year in Atlanta was his last with the Braves as a player. "After a dozen years of hitting to right-center, he became a dead-pull hitter and started swinging to put it out of the park. His batting average dropped but he led the league in home runs that year and the next."

Rather than hit to all fields, as he had done in Milwaukee County Stadium, Aaron became a pull hitter, connecting so often that Pat Jarvis dubbed Fulton County Stadium "the Launching Pad."

Henry Aaron picked up nicknames, too: writers and teammates called him "Hammerin' Hank" or "The Hammer," while opposing pitchers referred to him as "Bad Henry," a moniker created by Sandy Koufax and Don Drysdale because he was so good.

Although he was a notorious bad-ball hitter, he had such good plate discipline that he walked more often (1,402) than he struck out (1,383) during his 23-year career.

"Atlanta changed me as a hitter and a person at the same time," Aaron admitted in *I Had a Hammer*. "The real world made me angrier and hungrier than I had been as a young Milwaukee Brave. I was tired of being invisible. I was the equal of any ballplayer in the world, dammit, and if nobody was going to give me my due, it was time to grab for it."

He did just that, hitting his 400th home run against Philadelphia southpaw Bo Belinsky at Connie Mack Stadium on

April 20 and tying the record for most home runs through the end of June with 24.

Brother Tommie actually hit the first home run in the new ballpark, during an exhibition game against the Detroit Tigers. But Henry became the ballpark's chief beneficiary when the Braves took full occupancy of the facility a year later (the Braves played seven exhibition games in Atlanta during the 1965 season and drew 211,000 fans).

The first edition of the Atlanta Braves finished fifth but packed the new park, tripling the team's attendance during their last year in Milwaukee. But the fans didn't know how to behave.

"There was a novelty about the whole thing," Joe Torre told Bob Hope, author of *We Could've Finished Last Without You*. "At a game against the Giants, there were 45,000 fans in the stands and you could hear a pin drop. The fans didn't know what to do at a ballgame."

The first year in Dixie, Aaron's abilities somehow rubbed off on pitcher Tony Cloninger, who won 24 games during the last season in Milwaukee but then was left in too long during a dreary opening night game that went 13 innings. Never as good again on the mound, he still carved a niche in the history books by becoming the first *player* in National League history to hit two grand slams in one game.

A year later, another pitcher found his way out of obscurity as an emergency replacement. Phil Niekro, who had surfaced with Cloninger in Milwaukee, stepped out of the bullpen to baffle Philadelphia with a knuckleball that led to 318 wins and the Baseball Hall of Fame.

Aaron, Mathews, and Torre—also on that first Atlanta team—would later join him.

Few people realize that Aaron was a member of the Milwaukee Braves three seasons longer (1954–1965) than he played for the Atlanta Braves (1966–1974). But the race with Ruth that marked the closing years of his career clouded his earlier achievements.

The first Black Mobile native to reach the majors among a group that also included Billy Williams, Willie McCovey, Ozzie Smith, Cleon Jones, and Tommie Agee, Aaron was also the last player active in the Negro Leagues, which folded a few years after Jackie Robinson broke the baseball color line. He was also the first to introduce the Mobile stride style of hitting to the once all-white majors.

Aaron was sorry to see Eddie Mathews traded to the Houston Astros after the 1966 season, but the handwriting was on the wall when the team acquired fellow third baseman Clete Boyer, a far better defender, from the New York Yankees.

Nothing, however, could interfere with his power production. He led the league in home runs with 44 in 1966 and 39 in 1967, but would never win a home run crown again.

He still managed 44 homers—matching his uniform number for the fourth and final time—in 1969 and a career-best 47 two years later, when he knocked in 118 runs and had 162 hits in 139 games.

Counting his three home runs in the NLCS against the "Miracle" Mets in '69, Aaron actually authored his second 47-homer season. But those blasts went for naught, as the Braves lost three straight games at the start of the best-of-five series— the first scheduled pennant playoff in baseball history.

By then, the star right fielder already had his 500th homer, hit against Mike McCormick on July 14, 1968, and was on the verge of collecting his 3,000th hit, on May 17, 1970, in Cincinnati.

The first man with both 3,000 hits and 500 homers, he also became the first National Leaguer to produce a dozen 30-homer seasons.

In 1971, when he pulverized a Gaylord Perry pitch for his 600th home run on April 27, he was on his way toward another NL mark: most 40-homer seasons (7).

Even during the team's lean years, when it seemed like they were taking a beating every night, Hank Aaron stood like a mighty oak in a hurricane; he might bend but would never break.

He even survived a 1967 airplane fight with Rico Carty, a powerful Dominican outfielder who called himself "the Beeg Boy" but wasn't all that big when it came to mastering the art of outfield defense. When he first reached the Braves in 1964, the Braves paired him with Aaron as roommates on the road. It was not a match made in baseball heaven.

Three years later, in 1970, the team suffered its first losing season since leaving Boston. With a post-season ticket still unlikely in 1971, Aaron focused on catching Mays on the career home run list. He was 36 behind as the '71 campaign began.

As in Milwaukee, fan interest in Atlanta fell as the team floundered. Although Aaron was packing parks on the road, Fulton County Stadium wasn't much more than a mausoleum most nights in 1973, as Aaron approached Babe Ruth's record, and in 1974, after he passed it.

The Braves finished next-to-last in attendance both years, drawing a pathetic 800,655 in '73 as Aaron approached the record. High school football proved a bigger attraction to locals.

As he approached the record, the volume of media requests, marketing opportunities, and hate mail increased exponentially —a situation that complicated life for a quiet man who seemed to feel most comfortable out of the limelight but suddenly couldn't avoid it.

The tortoise—ignored as an unexciting plodder for most of his life—was finally sniffing the finish line.

Aaron was a guest star on television shows hosted by Dinah Shore, Merv Griffin, and Dean Martin; billboards promoting him popped up all over Atlanta; and Magnavox gave him a five-year, $1 million endorsement deal. He also became the first player to earn $200,000 in a season, signing a two-year contract for that amount in 1973, carrying him through his Atlanta career.

He was baseball royalty.

Before he finished his playing career with 755 home runs, Aaron said, "Ruth's homers are always going to be legend. Somebody can come along and hit 800 home runs and it's never going to mean as much as Babe Ruth's record. If I hit 750, it will just mean that Hank Aaron hit 750 home runs, that's all."

It wasn't easy for Aaron, who was hurt by the failure of the fans to support him, the failure of his first marriage, and the failure of the team to offer him a managerial or executive position with authority. He was also rattled by talk that the franchise might relocate again unless a local party could be found to revive it.

That's exactly what happened in 1976, Aaron's last year as a player, when he was back in Milwaukee with the Brewers but the Braves were purchased by innovative television magnate Ted Turner. It would be Turner who would not only transform the Braves into "America's team" after converting local station WCTG into the TBS SuperStation, but also bring Hank Aaron back as the highest-ranking Black executive in baseball history.

HOME RUN KING

A new downtown ballpark, built for the 1996 Summer Olympics in Atlanta, was named Turner Field after the man who saved the franchise. It served as the home of the Braves for 19 seasons.

CHAPTER 7

MEMORABLE MILESTONES

Hank Aaron had many milestones en route to 755 home runs over 23 seasons.

He hit 30 home runs in a season 15 times, 40 home runs eight times, 97 home runs against the Cincinnati Reds, and 17 home runs against a single pitcher—Hall of Famer Don Drysdale.

All told, Aaron homered against 310 pitchers in 31 different ballparks.

Aaron ripped his first home run on April 23, 1954, connecting against Cardinals right-hander Vic Raschi, who formerly pitched for the Yankees. It helped cement a 7–5 victory.

But his biggest and best home run—at least before No. 715— was the one he collected against Billy Muffett of the St. Louis Cardinals on September 23, 1957. The first home run Muffett surrendered all season, it came in the bottom half of the 11th inning at Milwaukee County Stadium.

The game was deadlocked at 2–2 with two outs when Aaron came up. Johnny Logan, who had singled, was on first. Aaron ended Muffett's homerless streak with a high drive to deep center.

Wally Moon leaped in vain, missing it by a few feet. Even Aaron initially thought Moon had snagged it.

"I remember looking at the clock," Aaron said later. "It showed 11:34 and that's when I hit the home run that won it for us. All the players grabbed me as I came across the plate and carried me off the field."

Aaron's jubilant teammates, celebrating their first National League pennant, were giving Aaron the same treatment Bobby Thomson received on October 3, 1951, after he hit "the shot heard 'round the world," winning the pennant for the New York Giants over the Brooklyn Dodgers.

"That was always my idea of the most important home run," the slugger said of Thomson's blast. "People were snake-dancing in Milwaukee that night and I woke up feeling like the King of Wisconsin."

He put a cherry on the championship cake with a .393 batting average that included three home runs in a seven-game World Series win against the New York Yankees. Aaron also hit three homers in the first National League Championship Series, in 1969 against the New York Mets. Aaron drove in seven of Atlanta's 15 runs in the three-game series. It was his last appearance in post-season play.

Always a dangerous hitter, Aaron hit nine home runs against Robin Roberts, eight against Juan Marichal, and an even dozen against Bob Friend, who lived up to his name.

He even hit three in a game for the only time in his career at San Francisco's Seals Stadium—a converted minor-league facility used by the Giants while Candlestick was built. That outburst—all two-run shots—came against three different pitchers as the Braves romped, 13–3.

Aaron didn't seem to care who was on the mound. He batted .342 against Steve Carlton, homering against him twice in one game on August 21, 1971. Aaron knocked in six of his team's runs in that 8–5 victory.

A month later, he connected in the 11th inning with two men on to cement a 7–5 victory over San Francisco.

Aaron delivered another extra-inning game-winner on June 13, 1972, with a one-out solo shot against future teammate Danny Frisella of the New York Mets in the 10th inning. The score was 6–5.

There were even a couple of homers that got away.

In the 16-inning game that pitted Warren Spahn against Marichal on July 2, 1963, Aaron actually hit a home run that was redirected by the howling gales common to Candlestick Park. But it was not Gone with the Wind.

According to eyewitness Eddie Mathews, who was sitting on the bench with an injury to his right wrist, "Aaron hit a ball that actually cleared the fence in left field but the wind brought it back and Willie McCovey caught it. Other than that, the closest we came to scoring was when Spahn hit a ball off the top of the fence in right. A foot higher and it was a home run."

Then there was the ball Aaron hit over the roof of Sportsman's Park in St. Louis. After Cardinals catcher Bob Uecker complained to umpire Chris Pelekoudas that Aaron's foot was out of the batter's box, the umpire nullified the homer and called Aaron out.

Uecker, a light-hitting backup who was watching from the dugout, was a past and future Aaron teammate whose main claim to fame as a player was a strange ability to handle Phil Niekro's knuckleball. After Aaron hit a high Curt Simmons change-up

450 feet into the heavy, humid air on August 18, 1965, Uecker immediately went ballistic, demanding that Pelekoudas call Aaron out because his left foot was outside the batter's box.

"It was the worst call I'd ever seen," Aaron complained afterward to The Associated Press. "I did the same thing before and popped up and the umpire didn't say a word. I always hit Simmons that way."

The Braves won the game, 5–3, on a Don Dillard pinch-homer in the ninth but protests by Aaron and Milwaukee manager Bobby Bragan fell upon deaf ears.

Although Babe Ruth had a reputation for gargantuan blasts, Aaron's balls were hardly cheap.

On June 18, 1962, he hit the longest home run of his career against a Mets pitcher named Jay Hook, a mechanical engineer who could explain the dynamics of a curveball but couldn't throw one.

Far from a pot-shot down the cozy lines in right or left field at the horseshoe-shaped Polo Grounds, that Aaron ball was a moon shot seven years before an astronaut set foot on the lunar surface. It went to the deepest part of the ballpark—bleacher seats that surrounded the center-field clubhouse, more than 500 feet from home plate. The last time that had happened was one night before, when Lou Brock of the Cubs connected, but the first time was years earlier, when Joe Adcock hit one for the Braves against the Giants before they moved to San Francisco.

"I just wanted to see if it could be done," Aaron quipped after the game. His titanic grand-slam cleared the bases and silenced newsmen who had asked Aaron whether he saw Brock's shot one night earlier.

That same season, Aaron delivered the only game-winning grand slam of his career. It happened on July 12, 1962, in a home game against the St. Louis Cardinals.

With veteran right-hander Larry Jackson nursing a 6–3 lead into the bottom of the ninth, Frank Bolling struck out. But pinch-hitter Tommie Aaron followed with a home run to left field and Roy McMillan singled, chasing Jackson in favor of closer Lindy McDaniel. Mack Jones greeted him with a single, bringing Eddie Mathews to the plate as the potential winning run. Even though Aaron was lurking in the on-deck circle, McDaniel walked Mathews.

Aaron then homered to left, finding almost the same spot his brother had found moments before, and the Braves walked off with an improbable 8–6 victory. It was the first time the brothers, who were also roommates, homered in the same game.

Although no one followed Hank Aaron around with a tape measure, some of his home runs looked like they were hit by Willie Stargell or Willie McCovey. In fact, Aaron and Earl Williams were the only players to reach the upper deck at Atlanta Fulton County Stadium.

Aaron home runs didn't always call for the tape measure. Many were line drives that whizzed past the ears of infielders, practically skimming the top the outfield grass before clearing the outfield fences.

Sometimes, Aaron had help from teammates when carving a niche in the record books. On June 8, 1961, for example, he teamed with Eddie Mathews, Joe Adcock, and Frank Thomas to become the first foursome to hit consecutive homers in a single inning, in a game at Cincinnati.

"One of the things I'm most proud of is my consistency," Aaron said. "Every day is a new day and every time you go the plate is a new time. That last time up is like reading yesterday's newspaper—it's gone."

He never won the coveted Triple Crown, encompassing league leadership in home runs, runs batted in, and batting average, but led the league in each of those three departments at least twice. Nor did he ever hit for the cycle, with a single, double, triple, and home run in the same game.

Dubbed "Hammerin' Hank" by long-time Braves executive Donald Davidson, an Aaron confidante who saw Hank Greenberg play, Aaron did some of his best work relatively late in his career.

His most unusual home run came on May 10, 1967, at Philadelphia's Connie Mack Stadium, an ancient edifice originally called Shibe Park. Facing Jim Bunning, one of those rare few pitchers who seemed to have his number, Aaron came to bat in the eighth inning with his team trailing, 3–1. With two men out and Mike de la Hoz on first, Aaron drove a Bunning delivery deep into center and over the head of Phillies center-fielder Don Lock.

By the time the 400-foot shot stopped rolling, Aaron had circled the bases for an inside-the-park home run—the only one of his career and the only four-bagger he ever hit against the future United States Senator. The Phils eventually won, 4–3, and Aaron answered with a regulation homer in the nightcap of that doubleheader, which the Braves won, 7–2.

On July 14, 1968, he celebrated Bastille Day by belting his 500th home run—exactly one year after Eddie Mathews had reached that figure. The second-youngest man to reach that milestone, he was especially proud to connect against Mike McCormick, a left-handed San Francisco starter who had won the Cy Young Award the previous season.

"I remember touching each base right in the center," he said of his home-run trot. "I'm glad it came in a victory because I wanted it to mean something and I'm glad it came against McCormick since he is an outstanding pitcher."

The Atlanta crowd that night, reported at 34,826, gave Aaron a loud and long ovation after the home run. "I got a tremendous thrill from their reaction," the slugger said. "I wanted to hit it in front of the fans who have been so good to me and the Braves."

Aaron admitted to pressing before producing No. 500. Because of the week-long interval between No. 499 and No. 500, Aaron said "I'm sorry you had to wait so long" to Braves chief executive Bill Bartholomay as he passed his box on the way back to the dugout.

Just over a year later, on July 31, the outfielder hit No. 537 to pass Mickey Mantle on the lifetime list and move into third place behind Babe Ruth and Willie Mays.

Aaron collected his 3,000th hit on May 17, 1970, against the Cincinnati Reds. Stan Musial, the last man in the 3,000 Hit Club, was at Crosley Field to congratulate him. Time was called so that the retired St. Louis superstar and Bartholomay hopped over a low fence, ran to first base, and offered their best wishes for continued success.

Henry answered quickly with a three-run homer (No. 570) in his next at-bat. He said later that he wanted his 3,000th to be a home run but was satisfied that it was a clean hit.

That single against Wayne Simpson made Aaron the first player with 3,000 hits and 500 home runs.

A feat of endurance, reaching 3,000 requires 20 years with at least 150 hits. Aaron did it in 17.

Then, on April 27, 1971, he joined Ruth and Mays as the only men with 600 home runs. It came in the third inning on the first pitch Gaylord Perry threw, clearing the fence and hitting high off the wall of the left-field grandstand. Ralph Garr, on base with an infield hit, scored ahead of him.

After connecting against his long-time nemesis, the thirty-seven-year-old Aaron told reporters, "I said all along I'd probably hit it off a pitcher I knew. I guessed fastball and got it. And I knew it was gone the minute I hit it.

"I read in the paper where Perry said I would have to earn it, so I worked that much harder. That statement perked me up."

Despite many previous meetings, Aaron had only connected once before on a Perry pitch—seven years earlier.

This time, the Giants won the game, 6–5 in 10 innings, when Mays singled in a run, but Aaron's historic shot thrilled some 13,494 fans in Atlanta Fulton County Stadium.

"I got a bigger thrill out of my 3,000th hit," Aaron admitted, "because I'd like to be remembered as a good all-around hitter and not just a fellow who hit home runs."

He finished that season with 47 homers, reaching the 40-homer plateau for the seventh time, a National League record. (Aaron and Bonds now share the NL record of eight.) His .669 slugging percentage was the best of his career.

Although a player strike shortened the 1972 campaign, Aaron passed Mays on the lifetime home run list, drove in the 2,000th run of his career, and erased Musial's mark for total bases. He finished the year with 673 career home runs and a clear shot at Babe Ruth's record. Also that season, he hit his 14th grand slam, tying the National League record for home runs with the bases loaded.

Still in remarkable shape for a man of his advanced athletic age, the thirty-nine-year-old Aaron was a study in concentration as the 1973 season began. The more hate mail he received, the more determined he became. He was even able to ignore a myriad of nagging injuries that would have sent a lesser man to the sidelines.

On July 21, he became the second man in baseball history with 700 home runs. The victim of his two-run, third-inning shot to left field in Atlanta was Philadelphia's Ken Brett, brother of three-time American League batting champ George Brett and a good hitter himself. (Brett went 2-for-3 in the same game to lift his batting average to .308.)

Unlike Jack Benny, the comedian who made a career out of prolonging his thirty-ninth birthday, Hank Aaron knew his days as an active player were numbered. He also knew he required more regular rest, which is why he had the fewest at-bats since his injury-shortened rookie year in 1954.

Aaron made the most of those opportunities, however. He hit 40 home runs in 392 at-bats, ending the 1973 season one short of Babe Ruth's record.

Jerry Reuss, then with the Houston Astros, yielded No. 713 on September 29, giving Aaron another day to tie the record. It didn't happen.

But the home run was Aaron's 40th, allowing him to create another record: first trio of teammates with simultaneous 40-homer seasons. Davey Johnson, who hit 43, and Darrell Evans, with 41, had gotten there previously.

"I don't know where Hank Aaron will break Ruth's record," said Atlanta manager Eddie Mathews at the time, "but I can tell you one thing: ten years from the day he hits it, three million people will say they were there."

HANK'S HISTORIC HOMERS				
HR#	Date	Opponent	Pitcher	Notes
1	23-04-1954	@ St. Louis Cardinals	Vic Raschi	First Career Home Run
100	15-08-1957	@ Cincinatti Reds	Don Gross	100th Home Run
109	23-09-1957	vs. St. Louis Cardinals	Billy Muffett	Won Pennant
200	03-07-1960	@ St. Louis Cardinals	Ron Kline	200th Home Run
300	19-04-1963	@ New York Mets	Roger Craig	300th Home Run
400	20-04-1966	@ Philadelphia Phillies	Bo Belinsky	400th Home Run
500	14-07-1968	vs. S.F. Giants	Mike McCormick	500th Home Run
600	27-04-1971	vs. S.F. Giants	Gaylord Perry	600th Home Run
661	06-08-1972	@ Cincinatti Reds	Don Gullett	2nd on All-Time Home Run List
700	21-07-1973	vs. Philadelphia Phillies	Ken Brett	700th Home Run
714	04-04-1974	@ Cincinatti Reds	Jack Billingham	Tied Babe Ruth
715	08-04-1974	vs. Los Angeles Dodgers	Al Downing	Passed Babe Ruth
733	02-10-1974	vs. Cincinnati Reds	Rawly Eastwick	Last NL Home Run
734	18-04-1975	@ Cleveland Indians	Gaylord Perry	First Career AL Home Run
755	20-07-1976	vs. California Angels	Dick Drago	Last Career Home Run

CHAPTER 8
AWARDS THAT WEREN'T

During his 23-year career in the major leagues, Hank Aaron rewrote the record book, posting more RBIs, total bases, and extra-base hits than anyone else, not to mention more home runs without artificial help.

But he won only one MVP Award and never even finished second.

He took the trophy in 1957, when he hit the extra-inning home run that gave the Milwaukee Braves their first pennant, but could also have won in 1956, 1958, 1969, 1971, and especially in 1959, when he turned in his finest season. He finished third in the voting in each of those seasons.

At least *The Sporting News*, the St. Louis–based tabloid that was then the sport's paper of record, tried to correct the injustice.

It named Aaron its Player of the Year in 1956 and 1963.

For years, Aaron was the best player in the game, though nobody seemed to know it. He heard people talk about the three center fielders who played for the New York teams before the Dodgers and Giants went west in 1958. Later, that trio was immortalized in song. Willie Mays, Mickey Mantle, and Duke

Snider may have had more charisma—and certainly more public recognition—but lacked both the numbers and the consistency of Hank Aaron.

So did other big names.

"I'd hear Willie Mays, Mickey Mantle, Harmon Killebrew, Roberto Clemente, and Frank Robinson," Aaron told author Ira Berkow, "but I'd never hear mine."

Hank Aaron started to change the script in 1956, his third season. At age twenty-two, he hit .328 to take his first batting title while also leading the league with 340 total bases and 200 hits. He was third in slugging and runs scored. But because the Braves finished one game behind Brooklyn in the final standings, Dodger pitching heroes Don Newcombe and Sal Maglie finished 1-2 in MVP voting. Newcombe, who had gone 27–7, also won the inaugural Cy Young Award, then given to only one pitcher in the major leagues.

Had Milwaukee not blown the one-game lead it took into the final weekend, Aaron might have won the MVP in 1956.

A low-key player in a small-market city, even Hank Aaron had trouble putting Milwaukee on the major-league map. When the Braves finally won a pennant in 1957, Mantle himself dubbed the town "Bushville" because the star center fielder considered Wisconsin unsophisticated, almost unworthy of representing the National League in the World Series against the powerful Yankees. Milwaukee had only been in the major leagues for four years and had always played bridesmaid behind the Dodgers and Giants—the perennial powers who shared the stage in the nation's biggest city.

Aaron couldn't be denied in 1957, when he hit the pennant-winning home run against St. Louis reliever Billy Muffett, and finished with NL highs in hits, home runs, total bases, and RBIs. Even that year, however, the voting was close. Aaron finished with 239 votes to Stan Musial's 230.

Aaron would not win the trophy again—even though his performance in some of the years that followed was even more impressive.

And let's not overlook one of the biggest snubs of all: the World Series MVP Award in 1957. Aaron led both teams with a .393 batting average, three home runs, and seven RBIs as the Braves pulled out a seven-game upset. He even homered against Don Larsen, who had thrown the only perfect game in World Series history one year earlier.

But the writers awarded the MVP—a brand-new Chevrolet—to Lew Burdette, whose three complete-game wins over the Yankees included a pair of shutouts. But Aaron himself was feeling shut out when that award was announced.

In fact, every time an award Aaron thought he had earned instead went to a white player, Aaron wondered whether racism had entered into the voting—especially since the national media was overwhelmingly white during his heyday.

The 1959 season was probably the best of Aaron's career. He hit .355 with 223 hits and 400 total bases—all league highs—and ranked third in both home runs (39) and RBIs (123). But all that netted the young outfielder was a third-place finish in the voting, trailing Cubs shortstop Ernie Banks and Braves teammate Eddie Mathews, who led the NL with 46 home runs.

Even with Banks, the first National Leaguer to win consecutive MVPs, the Cubs could not produce a winning season, finishing 74–80 to wind up sixth in the eight-team league. The year before, they were fifth but only 72–82. But the affable Banks, popular with the press, beat out Mays for the trophy, with Aaron finishing third.

Off to the best start of his career, Aaron hit .508 in April and was still hitting .487 on May 14. As late as Memorial Day, the average stood at .461—and stayed above .400 until June 16. "He has become a better hitter than ever because he's gotten more confidence," said Rogers Hornsby, who once hit .424. "He hits with power to all fields and pays more attention to the strike zone."

Then there was 1963, when Aaron came within a whisker of an elusive Triple Crown, last won in the National League by Joe Medwick in 1937. Aaron's 44 homers and 130 RBIs led the league, yet his .319 batting average placed third, and in doing so became the first player with 40 home runs and 30 stolen bases in the same season. For good measure, his 30/30 season—the only one of his career—was the third in baseball history. Aaron also paced the circuit in total bases (370), runs scored (121), and slugging (.586).

Unfortunately for Aaron, the Dodgers won the pennant and the writers decided the MVP award should go to their star pitcher, Sandy Koufax, after he went 25–5, fanned 306 hitters, posted a 1.88 ERA, and threw 11 shutouts—including a no-hitter. Dick Groat was runner-up, with Aaron again third.

Aaron, who hit .362 against Koufax in his career, homering against him seven times, would wind up third in the MVP balloting twice more, in 1969 and 1971.

Historians remember 1969 as the year Richard Nixon moved into the Oval Office, Neil Armstrong walked on the moon, and the Miracle Mets roared from ninth place to a world championship that also defied all odds.

That same year the National League expanded, adding the Montreal Expos and San Diego Padres, and split into two six-team divisions. Although the Braves wound up in the West, putting them into direct conflict with the Los Angeles Dodgers and San Francisco Giants, they rode Aaron's bat to the title—their first finish in first place since the Milwaukee Braves won the pennant in '57.

For Hank Aaron, who got both All-Star and MVP votes every year from 1955–1973, it was a typical year.

He again matched his uniform number with 44 home runs, added 97 RBIs, and hit an even .300. It was a great season, followed by home runs in each of the three Championship Series games against the Mets, but Aaron's efforts weren't enough to convince MVP voters. They gave the trophy to San Francisco slugger Willie McCovey, whose .320 average and league-leading 45 homers and 126 RBIs all topped Aaron's output, even though his Giants trailed the Braves by three games at season's end. Tom Seaver, who won 25 games for the Mets, was his runner-up.

By 1971, Aaron was plowing through a plethora of baseball records, which were falling like dominoes under a bulldozer. He got his 3,000th hit in 1970 but was even better in '71, which some insiders consider his best season.

At age thirty-seven, the great power-hitter was showing signs of slowing down. His knee, injured in a home-plate collision with Giants catcher Dick Dietz, was barking, his arm strength was waning, and he no longer had the speed of his youth.

But his bat speed was still there, since statistics don't lie. He not only became the third player to hit 600 home runs but led the team with 47 home runs—a career high—and 118 RBIs. His batting average was .327, fifth in the league, but his best since

1964, when he finished a point higher in the next-to-last season of the Milwaukee Braves.

Former teammate Joe Torre, who won the batting title with the St. Louis Cardinals, was the surprise MVP winner over Willie Stargell, whose 48 homers led the league, and Aaron. Although his Cardinals finished second, Torre was first in batting average but also hits, runs, and total bases. The former catcher, who made a smooth transition to third base, got hot and stayed hot, hitting 66 points above his previous lifetime average to finish at .363, easily the best mark of his career.

Two years later, Aaron hit the 700th home run en route to his final 40-homer campaign. When he finished with exactly that number, he joined teammates Davey Johnson and Darrell Evans as the first trio of teammates to hit that many in the same season.

By then, Aaron had passed Willie Mays for second on the career home run list and was clearly in position to challenge the ghost of Babe Ruth . . . yet MVP voters weren't swayed.

He finished only 12th, far behind winner Pete Rose, the switch-hitting Cincinnati leadoff man, but the baseball world was becoming increasingly aware of him.

For Aaron, who had labored in obscurity far too long, the recognition was long overdue.

When baseball celebrated its 100th anniversary at a banquet in a Washington hotel just before the 1969 All-Star Game at RFK Stadium, the outfielders selected by the media to the all-time outfield of living players were Ted Williams, Joe DiMaggio, and Willie Mays.

"That wasn't so bad," said Aaron, an All-Star more often than any other player, "but I wasn't even invited to the dinner."

When the Midsummer Classic moved to Cincinnati the following July, Aaron's hotel reservation was misplaced. "We have nothing in your name and we've never heard of you," the desk clerk told him.

At All-Star time, Aaron invariably deserved a spot in the National League's starting lineup, but didn't always get one. Even when he did, he sometimes had to shift from right field to left to accommodate the flashier Clemente.

Though selected to 25 All-Star Games, Aaron made only 14 starts in right field, one in left field, one in center field, and one at first base. On *eight separate occasions*, Hank Aaron was riding the pine when the All-Star Game started. Talk about snubs!

Even President Nixon struck out in dealing with Aaron— twice. He once sent him a holiday greeting card addressed to "Frank" Aaron and later sent a congratulatory telegram, after his 700th home run, to the Braves Booster Club rather than the Braves Baseball Club.

Bowie Kuhn, then the Commissioner of Baseball, didn't send a wire—or even show up to witness Aaron's 715th home run, an event fans voted "Most Memorable Moment" in baseball history, on April 8, 1974. But Kuhn invoked the "best interests of baseball" clause after the Braves balked at playing Aaron in the 1974 season-opening road series in Cincinnati. Atlanta, hoping for a sell-out at its stadium, wanted him to break Babe Ruth's record at home a few days later.

Aaron also felt slighted by his hometown fans. They packed the park during the last week of the 1973 season and the first home game of 1974, but disappeared the minute the record fell—even leaving in droves after Aaron delivered the historic hit in the fourth inning.

When he joined Stan Musial as the only living player to collect 3,000 hits in 1970, Aaron immediately sent the ball to the National Baseball Hall of Fame. Rather than display it right away, the ball wound up buried in the basement archives.

Race probably contributed to some of the perceived slights. According to Berkow, Aaron believed the white press wanted to promote white players—at his expense.

As late as the spring of 1974, when Aaron was on the verge of becoming the game's new home run king, an Atlanta newspaper diminished the achievement in an article headlined, "The Truth About Ruth."

It said, "While Braves right fielder Hank Aaron will probably break Ruth's home run record this year, no one has yet come close to matching the magnetism of the Babe."

Say what?

"The thing about Hank," Eddie Mathews told Berkow, "is that he does everything so effortlessly, so expressionlessly. He runs as hard as he has to. His hat doesn't fly off the way Mays's did. Clemente ran and looked like he was falling apart at the seams. Aaron runs with the shaft let out but you'd never know it. Yet when the smoke clears, he's standing there in the same place as the others."

The late Milo Hamilton, who served as voice of the Braves when the team relocated to Atlanta in 1966, once ran afoul of the slugger regarding an apparent misinterpretation by *Atlanta Journal* reporter Wilt Browning.

"Aaron, Mays, and Clemente were the starting outfielders," Hamilton wrote in his autobiography *Making Airwaves*. "Walter Alston asked Aaron if he would play left. So at the luncheon I said that for the All-Star Game, Clemente was the right-fielder.

I didn't say he was the greatest right-fielder or that he had forced Aaron to move to left (the manager did that). Unbeknownst to me, Wilt Browning, the beat writer for the *Atlanta Journal*, went from that luncheon to the ballpark and told Aaron that I had introduced Clemente as the greatest right-fielder. It simply was not true.

"If Aaron would have asked me about it directly, I could have straightened things out. If necessary, I'd have brought Bob Prince and Danny Murtaugh over there and said, 'Will you tell him what I said?' By that time, it was too late for me to address it with Aaron and Browning had written a story. Thankfully, Donald Davidson, a very close confidant of Aaron, told Henry, 'You know he didn't say that.' Davidson got us together and it was a closed issue. And that was the end of it."

Years later, Hamilton served as the emcee of the on-the-field festivities honoring Aaron for breaking Babe Ruth's record on April 8, 1974.

Major League Baseball tried to repair the damage done to Aaron's psyche by lack of recognition over the years by creating the Hank Aaron Award on April 8, 1999—the 25th anniversary of his 715th home run.

Given annually to the best offensive performer in each league, the award is decided by a panel of Hall of Famers in conjunction with a nationwide fan vote.

The first recipients were Manny Ramirez and Sammy Sosa, though Alex Rodriguez won the award four times, more than any other player.

CHAPTER 9
PERPETUAL ALL-STAR

Henry Aaron was an All-Star 25 times, more than anyone else, but appeared 24 times, a record shared by Willie Mays and Stan Musial, because he missed the first of two All-Star Games in 1962 with an injury. He made the team in every one of his 23 seasons in the majors except his first, when he played for the Milwaukee Braves, and his last, when he played for the Milwaukee Brewers.

Because inter-league play did not begin until 1997, long after he left the game, Aaron struggled against American League pitchers he hadn't seen previously. Of course, they hadn't seen him either, but word spreads fast among the brethren of the pitching fraternity.

In his first All-Star Game, in front of a hometown crowd at Milwaukee County Stadium in 1955, Aaron was one of four Braves selected, along with catcher Del Crandall, shortstop Johnny Logan, and pitcher Gene Conley.

Though not chosen to start, Aaron entered as a pinch-runner for Don Mueller, stayed in to play right field, and singled in both of his plate appearances. One of those hits knocked in a run—the margin of victory in a 6–5, 12-inning National League victory.

Conley, who struck out the side in the ninth inning, picked up the win.

For Aaron, it would be the only time he collected more than one hit in an All-Star Game. He had a fleeting moment of glory, however, in one of the two 1959 games, when he singled in the tying run in the eighth inning, scoring the winning marker on a triple by Willie Mays.

Every year, fans and media expected great things from Aaron at the All-Star Game, electing him to start almost every year of his career.

One notable exception was 1957, when fans in small-market Cincinnati somehow stuffed the ballot box, electing seven of eight Reds regulars plus Cardinals superstar Stan Musial. Angry baseball commissioner Ford Frick vetoed their choices of Wally Post and Gus Bell, inserting Aaron and Willie Mays into the NL lineup and stripping the fans of their right to pick All-Star lineups.

He introduced a more objective selection system in 1958, with lineups determined by vote of players, coaches, and managers, each of whom could vote just once and could not vote for teammates. That system worked well until then-commissioner Bowie Kuhn, seizing a commercial opportunity, returned the vote to the fans with computerized ballots distributed in ballparks. The process quickly evolved into a popularity contest but did not hurt Hank Aaron.

Respected and beloved around the majors, his name was almost automatic—even though his production in the Midsummer Classic was rather anemic. He finished with 13 hits in 67 at-bats, resulting in an unbecoming All-Star Game batting average of .194, but saved his heroics for his final years.

Hall of Famer Charlie Gehringer, a Hall of Fame second baseman, threw out the first pitch of the All-Star Game played at ancient Tiger Stadium on July 13, 1971. He did better than some of the actual pitchers who followed.

Reggie Jackson hit a shot off the light tower in right-center field that might have been the longest home run in All-Star history, perhaps traveling as far as 540 feet. Frank Robinson became the first man to hit All-Star homers for both leagues. And Hank Aaron, after topping the fan vote to select the lineups, hit a line drive to the upper deck in right field despite a knee problem that caused his departure after that inning.

The victim of his first All-Star homer was Vida Blue, the hard-throwing rookie left-hander of the Oakland A's. The first extra-base hit in Aaron's long All-Star log, it came in Aaron's 59th All-Star at-bat and 65th plate appearance.

The very next year, with the Midsummer Classic moving to his home turf in Atlanta, the future home run king struck again.

Timed to coincide with the city's 125th birthday, the game provided an excuse for merchants to dress mannequins in baseball uniforms, civic leaders to post 1,000 celebratory banners, and greeters to paste 10,000 All-Star Game lapel stickers on airport arrivals. A massive street festival went off without a hitch at Peachtree Center.

Once the game started, neither team did much damage at the plate. But that was before Hank Aaron thrilled the Atlanta faithful by feasting on the first pitch thrown by Gaylord Perry, the former San Francisco star who had already won 16 games that season for the Cleveland Indians en route to the American League's Cy Young Award.

Perry, who had previously surrendered Aaron's 600th home run, delivered a pitch just off the plate but close enough for the slugger to hit with authority. The drive put the Nationals ahead, 2–1, and drove the fans into a frenzy.

Aaron was pretty excited too after delivering a game-changing home run in the first All-Star Game hosted by the Braves in Atlanta and the first for the franchise since 1955.

"I was flying," he told reporters afterward. "It was a great feeling."

The perennial All-Star had an even better feeling after taking his position in right field for the top of the seventh. National League manager Danny Murtaugh, who had come out of retirement to run the NL All-Stars, called time and sent Al Oliver out to replace Aaron in right field. He ran in alone, preoccupied with the thought that he could actually accomplish the unthinkable and catch Babe Ruth.

His sixth-inning drive had delighted 53,107 denizens of Atlanta Fulton County Stadium and triggered one of five standing ovations for the hometown superstar on that overcast night, disappearing over the 375-foot marker in left-center and scoring Cesar Cedeno from first base.

It not only put the National League ahead, 2–1, in the 43rd Midsummer Classic but also prompted media members to vote him All-Star MVP honors for the first time. The honor, however, would be short-lived.

Pinch-hitter Cookie Rojas, an unlikely power source, delivered a two-run, eighth-inning homer against Bill Stoneman, giving the American League a 3–2 lead.

After the NL knotted the score in the ninth against knuckleballer Wilbur Wood on hits by Billy Williams and Manny

Sanguillen, coupled with a fielder's choice, the Senior Circuit won the game in 10 innings on a walk to pinch-hitter Nate Colbert, who moved to second on a sacrifice by Chris Speier, and then scored on a single to right-center by Joe Morgan against Dave McNally. The 4–3 win was the ninth in ten years for the National League.

Morgan, given the MVP trophy first awarded to Aaron, said later, "When Aaron hit the homer, it was like watching a Hollywood movie. I thought he should have been the hero. Then when Rojas hit his, I said, 'Gee, it's not supposed to be that way.'"

Rojas, a thirty-three-year-old second baseman not known for his power, had played all nine positions in professional baseball but was known more for speed, defense, and versatility than long-ball production (hitting just 54 home runs in his 16-year career). Still, at least for the moment, he tarnished Hank Aaron's star.

"I thought we were going to win it," he said of the American League All-Stars. "At first I thought [my shot] would be caught but when I rounded first base, I saw it was out. Then I thought I only needed 630 more to catch Hank Aaron."

Aaron wound up as runner-up to Morgan in the writers' poll, followed by winning pitcher Tug McGraw, who worked the last two innings, and Rojas.

"That has to be my most dramatic home runs for two reasons," said Aaron, who connected at 9:54 p.m. EST. "First, I haven't had good luck in All-Star Games. And then there are the fans. The people in Atlanta have been great to me. They came to see me hit one and I was pleased I came through.

"If I was to have a good All-Star Game, I'm glad it came in Atlanta for the fans."

Perry, the opposing pitcher, had faced Aaron before. In fact, he threw the ball that became the slugger's 600th home run.

"I felt comfortable hitting against Perry," he said. "The pitch I hit off him was a spitter. It wasn't one of his best spitters, but it was a spitter. It was a fast spitter, one that broke down and in on me. He doesn't fool me with many of his spitters."

Even a home run against an illegal pitch counts—especially considering the setting.

"All-Star Games are very special to me," Aaron said before the game. "They always have been. And I hope I never lose my feeling for them.

"Some guys have said they'd rather have the days off. You know, go visit their family, hunt, fish, or do something else.

"I respect their feelings but honestly can't understand it. I mean it's one of the highest honors in baseball to be chosen to play in the game. Or at least I feel it is."

At age thirty-eight, Aaron opened the game in the NL outfield after topping the fan voting for the second consecutive season. He got 3,126,694 votes out of 3,171,556 cast.

"I'll always be grateful to the fans for that honor," said the soft-spoken slugger. "And THE home run will be hard to forget."

Despite an atypical .256 batting average going into the All-Star Game, Aaron felt he had a right to start.

"I certainly do," he said when asked by a reporter. "This season has been awfully up and down for me and I haven't been as consistent as I would like to be. I had anticipated having a higher batting average, but my home runs are up and I feel the average will be climbing soon. Or at least I hope it will."

Aaron started the 1972 All-Star Game in right field, his normal position. He also batted in his customary third spot in the lineup.

But his ineptitude in past All-Star play remained a puzzlement. "I really can't explain why I haven't gotten a home run before last year," he said, "and can't explain why I haven't hit any better in All-Star Games either. Maybe their pitching is better than ours. I honestly don't know."

CHAPTER 10

TERRIFIC TEAMMATES

They could have had their own book.

Aaron, Mathews, and Spahn might have been the title.

Warren Spahn got there first, in 1942, when Casey Stengel was managing the Boston Braves and Bob Feller was in the process of winning his eight battle stars as wartime tail-gunner on the USS *Alabama*.

Spahn didn't win in his debut but did aggravate Stengel by refusing to retaliate when a Brooklyn pitcher hit one of the Boston Braves. Accusing the left-hander of having no guts, Stengel shipped him back to the minor leagues.

He returned in time to win at least 20 games in 13 different seasons, to notch 363 victories and 363 base-hits, and to reunite with Stengel in New York when both were well-over-the-hill. During their days with the hapless Mets in 1965, Spahn said, "I played for Casey before and after he was a genius."

While Stengel was winning 10 pennants in 12 years with the Yankees, from 1949–1960, Spahn was winning more games than any left-handed pitcher in the history of baseball—not to mention more games than any pitcher after the end of World War II.

He even homered for the Braves in 17 consecutive seasons—a feat also accomplished only by Aaron and Chipper Jones, two other Hall of Famers. Because he could hit, Spahn was seldom lifted for a pinch-hitter. In fact, he was often *used* as a pinch-hitter.

Spahn was twenty-five when he notched his first career victory, making his record even more striking, but he worked in the days of a four-man rotation and no pitch counts. The only ballplayer to win a battlefield commission in the Second World War, Spahn had more complete games (382) than victories.

One of those complete games, on July 2, 1963, was a 16-inning, 1–0 defeat at wind-blown Candlestick Park in San Francisco. Both Spahn and opposing pitcher Juan Marichal—nearly twenty years his junior—threw more than 200 pitches until Willie Mays ended the marathon with a solo home run in the 16th inning.

The box score doesn't show it, but Hank Aaron almost ended the game earlier—before the whipping wind, blowing in from left field, held up a likely home run ball long enough for left-fielder (Willie McCovey) to catch it.

Years later, when Major League Baseball revealed its Team of the Century at the 1999 All-Star Game in Boston, Spahn and Marichal recalled the epic pitching duel.

According to Spahn, Braves manager Bobby Bragan was going to lift him for a pinch-hitter in the 10th inning before the pitcher talked him out of it. "As long as that young guy's out there, I'm staying in," Spahn told him.

"That's pretty funny," Marichal responded. "Our manager, Alvin Dark, was going to bat for me too. And I told him, 'As long as that old man is out there, I'm going to stay out there too.'"

Throwing so many pitches at such an advanced athletic age (forty-two) might have deprived Spahn of a chance to join Cy Young and Walter Johnson as 400-game winners.

Although he finished the 1963 season with a 23–7 record, seven shutouts, and a 2.60 ERA, he failed to defy Father Time any further. Even though he wound up on the cover of the prestigious *Street & Smith's Baseball Yearbook* the following February, the old man turned old in a hurry.

"It happened all of a sudden with Spahn," Aaron wrote in *I Had a Hammer*, the autobiography he wrote with Lonnie Wheeler. "We should have been expecting it because he was forty-three years old but he had been so good for so long that we couldn't fathom him doing anything else but winning.

"He finally hit the wall in 1964. He still looked like himself, with the fancy wind-up and big leg lick, but there was nothing left on the ball. He wound up with a record of 6–13.

"The sad part about it was that we might have won the pennant in 1964 if he'd been even a shadow of the old Spahn because after years of searching for young pitchers, we found Tony Cloninger and Denny Lemaster. We finished fifth but only five games behind the Cardinals."

Traditionally a slow starter, Spahn had opened the '64 season with a 5–4 record but was suddenly hit so hard that he was taken out of the rotation after the All-Star break. His pride stung, the pitcher complained bitterly. But he won only one more game in a Milwaukee uniform.

Insisting he could still pitch, Spahn became a player-coach for Casey Stengel's 1965 Mets, who had also reactivated catching great Yogi Berra. "I don't know if we'll be the oldest battery in baseball history," Spahn said, "but we'll certainly be the ugliest."

Not as ugly as his numbers in 1965, his final season: 4–12 for the Mets, where he was officially a player-coach, and 3–4 with San Francisco after the Giants signed him in the hopes of a last hurrah. But he was toast.

Spahn wasn't the only culprit. Aaron even admitted he didn't have a big year either—at least by his own lofty standards. He hit .328 but homered just 24 times—20 less than his total from the previous season.

"A little more power from me might well have made the difference because we were starting to put together another potent lineup," Aaron wrote in his book.

Mathews also did not deliver as expected. After leading the National League with 46 home runs in 1959, when the Braves tied the Dodgers before dropping an unscheduled best-of-three pennant playoff, his once-prolific power declined five years in a row.

In order, he had 39, 32, 29, 23, and 23 home runs from 1960–1964, and his batting average fell to a career-worst .233 in '64. A handsome matinee idol once billed as the second coming of Babe Ruth, Mathews was a fiery competitor who got into more than his share of fights—on the field, in a night spot, or anywhere someone offered a dissenting opinion.

A proud and outspoken star, he complained when Bobby Bragan platooned him, benching the left-handed hitter against left-handed pitchers. The day he replaced Bragan, on August 9, 1966, Billy Hitchcock put Mathews into the lineup against Sandy Koufax, the best lefty in the league, and received an instant reward: Mathews homered in the ninth inning of a 1–1 pitching duel between Koufax and young Denny Lemaster. The fans loved it.

Courtesy of the National Baseball Hall of Fame and Museum.

During a career that included 23 major-league seasons, Hank Aaron hit more home runs, collected more runs batted in, and made more All-Star teams than anyone else in baseball history before he retired after the 1976 season. The last major-leaguer who played in the Negro Leagues, he desegregated the South as a minor-leaguer in the Sally League and later became the biggest black star on the first team to call Dixie home. *Courtesy of the Fiorentino Collection, reprinted with permission of artist James Fiorentino.*

 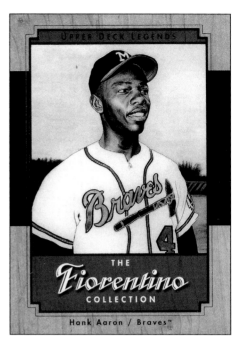

A middle infielder when signed by the Boston Braves, Henry Aaron found fame and fortune after switching to the outfield as a rookie with the 1954 Milwaukee Braves. *Courtesy of the Fiorentino Collection, reprinted with permission of artist James Fiorentino.*

En route to MVP honors in the 1953 Sally League, Hank Aaron thanks Jacksonville pilot Ben Geraghty, the man he later called the best manager he ever had. Aaron reached the majors with the Milwaukee Braves a year later. *Getty Images.*

The wiry Aaron became a power hitter after abandoning the cross-handed stance he used in the minors. *Courtesy of the Fiorentino Collection, reprinted with permission of artist James Fiorentino.*

The Aaron brothers, Hank (44) and Tommie (28), first joined forces with the 1962 Milwaukee Braves and homered in the same game three times. *Getty Images.*

After the Milwaukee Braves beat the New York Yankees for the 1957 World Championship, the major awards went to Aaron, the National League's Most Valuable Player, and teammate Warren Spahn, who captured the Cy Young Award given to the game's best pitcher. It was the only time either of them won those honors and the only year Milwaukee won the World Series. *Getty Images.*

Hank Aaron won the only MVP award of his career after his home run won the pennant for the 1957 Milwaukee Braves. A quiet star playing out of the media spotlight, he never finished better than third in any other MVP balloting.

When rain claimed a late-September game as Hank Aaron neared Babe Ruth's record in 1973, the slugger shared a clubhouse laugh with Georgia Governor Jimmy Carter (right) and visiting Governor Sherman Tribbitt of Delaware (center). Directly behind Aaron's right shoulder is author Dan Schlossberg, then twenty-five, who had been interviewing the slugger when the governors interrupted. *Getty Images.*

President George W. Bush presented Hank Aaron with the Presidential Medal of Freedom Award during a July 9, 2002 ceremony at the White House. The medal is the highest civilian award given to those who have made meritorious contributions to the security or national interests of the United States, to world peace, or to cultural or other significant public or private endeavors. *Getty Images.*

Often compared to fellow superstar Willie Mays, shown here at the 1973 All-Star Game in Kansas City, Aaron also had a friendly rivalry with Eddie Mathews (41), combining to hit a record 863 home runs during the time they were teammates. *Photos by Dan Schlossberg.*

Dusty Baker, taking a break from this 1974 interview with Dan Schlossberg, was just beginning his career as Hank Aaron was winding down. *Courtesy of Dan Schlossberg.*

Dan Schlossberg interviews Hank Aaron at Jarry Parc in 1969, the year the Montreal Expos joined the National League. *Courtesy of Dan Schlossberg.*

Hank Aaron took time to visit with former teammate George Stone of the Mets before a game at Shea Stadium. *Photo by Dan Schlossberg.*

Hank Aaron, talking here with future author Dan Schlossberg at Montreal's Jarry Parc, perfected the art of signing autographs and answering questions simultaneously. *Courtesy of Dan Schlossberg.*

On April 8, 1974, Atlanta Braves slugger Hank Aaron hit home run No. 715 against Dodgers lefty Al Downing (44) as second baseman Davey Lopes (15) watched. The fourth-inning shot broke Babe Ruth's career home run record. Joe Ferguson was behind the plate for Los Angeles. *Getty Images.*

Hank Aaron's mother Estella gave her favorite home hitter a hug after Hammerin' Hank made Babe Ruth an also-ran, turning an Al Downing pitch into his 715th career homer. The ball was snagged in the Braves bullpen by relief pitcher Tom House. *Getty Images.*

After 20 years and nearly 3,000 games, The Great Chase finally ended for Hank Aaron. He and new wife Billye seemed relieved at a post-game news conference in Atlanta Fulton County Stadium. *Getty Images.*

I was there when Hank Aaron hit his 714th career home run to tie Babe Ruth as the top home run hitter in the history of Baseball.

Date _____

Place _____

I was there when Hank Aaron hit his 715th career home run to pass Babe Ruth as the top home run hitter in the history of Baseball.

Date _April 8, 1974_

Place _Atlanta Stadium_

Hoping he would tie and top Babe Ruth at home, the Atlanta Braves printed certificates to suit both occasions. But those for No. 714 became phantoms when Hank homered against Jack Billingham in his first at-bat on Opening Day in Cincinnati. When the Braves returned home after the three-game road series, he broke the record in his first home game, on April 8, 1974. *Courtesy of the Ron Visco Collection.*

For most of his career, Atlanta went to spring training at West Palm Beach Municipal Stadium, a South Florida facility they shared with the Montreal Expos, now the Washington Nationals. *Photo by Dan Schlossberg.*

A Florida license plate celebrates the successful end of the chase. *Photo by Dan Schlossberg.*

As good with a camera as he was with a bat, Hank Aaron took pictures of family members in front of his Hall of Fame plaque. *Getty Images.*

No player has a bigger exhibit in the Baseball Hall of Fame than Hank Aaron's Chasing the Dream, opened in 2010. *Photo by Jean Fruth.*

Since baseball is a game of memorable numbers, none are bigger than the 44 worn by Hank Aaron and the 755 home runs hit by the star slugger. They seem larger than life at CoolToday Park, the North Port, FL facility where the Braves hold spring training, and Truist Park, their regular-season home in Atlanta. *Photos by Dan Schlossberg.*

Hank Aaron in 2002 at New York's Museum of Natural History, where the Baseball as America exhibit featured a display case with his picture and jersey. *Photo by Mile E. Stewart Jr.*

The city-owned boyhood home of Hank Aaron in Mobile, AL was built by his father Herbert in 1942 but later became an Aaron museum adjacent to Hank Aaron Stadium. The ballpark opened in 1997 as home of the Southern League's Mobile BayBears but closed when the franchise moved to Madison in 2020. The home now sits in James Seals Park south of downtown. *Photo by Jean Fruth.*

Hank Aaron donned a Braves jersey again to throw out the first pitch to fellow Hall of Famer Bobby Cox, long-time manager of the Braves, when Truist Park opened in 2017. *Photo by Jean Fruth.*

Although he never earned more than $240,000 a year as a player, Henry Aaron made millions post-retirement as an entrepeneur with wise investments in automobile dealerships, restaurants, and fast food franchises. He also cultivated a reputation as a civil rights advocate who campaigned for presidents and befriended fellow Atlanta residents Jimmy Carter, Martin Luther King Jr., Anthony Young, and Ralph David Abernathy. *Photo by Jean Fruth.*

But Mathews remained a falling star.

He peaked too early, collecting 47 homers and 137 RBIs—both personal highs—in 1953, the franchise's first year in Milwaukee. He never won an MVP Award but twice finished second in the voting.

"For the first thirteen years of my career," Aaron once said, "Eddie Mathews was ahead of me in home runs. A lot of people thought if anyone was going to break Babe Ruth's career record, it was going to be him."

But even Aaron noticed the decline of Mathews as a power source in the Atlanta lineup. "When Eddie left before the 1967 season—and even earlier when his power was diminishing—I decided I had to become more of a power-hitter. I consciously changed my swing and concentrated on pulling the ball to left field. Until then, I was more of a straightaway hitter and a good percentage of my home runs went to right field.

"Of course the move from Milwaukee County Stadium to Atlanta Stadium, a much cozier park for [right-handed] home run hitters, didn't hurt me either."

Combined with Aaron, however, Mathews was half of the best home run tandem in baseball history. During the time they were teammates, starting with Aaron's arrival in 1954 and the trade of Mathews during the winter of 1966, the pair pounded 863 home runs, a handful more than the totals of Babe Ruth and Lou Gehrig (859) or Willie Mays and Willie McCovey (801).

Before Mike Schmidt finally passed him, Mathews had more home runs than any third baseman in baseball history. He also held the single-season mark before Schmidt hit one more.

The only man to play for, coach, and manage the Braves, Mathews was also the only man to play for the team in all three of its homes: Boston, Milwaukee, and Atlanta. He left only after Paul Richards decided he wanted better defense from the position and acquired Clete Boyer from the New York Yankees.

Less than a year later, Mathews, pitcher Arnie Umbach, and minor-league infielder Sandy Alomar were moved to Houston for the forgettable tandem of pitcher Bob Bruce and Dave Nicholson, a strikeout-prone outfielder. Neither contributed much to the Braves, but Mathews helped the 1968 Detroit Tigers win a World Series while Alomar went on to have a long and distinguished career.

To compound the felony, Mathews found out about the trade when a reporter called to ask for his reaction. The team never told him. Then it spelled his name wrong in the official press release. That was no way to treat a future Hall of Famer.

Unlike Mathews, who said he was shocked by his trade, Aaron wanted to finish his career where it started: in Milwaukee.

Like Willie Mays, who started and ended in New York (but with different teams), Aaron got his wish. The Braves sent him to the Brewers for outfielder Dave May and pitcher Roger Alexander. May hit 15 home runs over two seasons in Atlanta before continuing his career elsewhere, but Alexander never reached the majors.

Two years later, Aaron retired with the most home runs (755), the most RBIs (2,297), the most extra-base hits (1,477), and the most total bases (6,856). A .305 lifetime hitter, he ranked second in at-bats (12,364), runs (2,174), and third in games (3,298) and hits (3,771). He was seventh in years of service (23), eighth in doubles (624), and 11th in singles (2,294).

The first member of the 500 Home Run Club to also have 3,000 hits, he had a 30/30 season, won three Gold Gloves, and was a first-ballot selection to the National Baseball Hall of Fame. He even made a small fortune from the syndicated television show *Home Run Derby*, which once pitted him against Mathews. In 1959, for example, Aaron's $30,000 winnings were nearly twice as much as his baseball salary in that non-union era.

Aaron's statistics were staggering. Consider the fact that his total bases record still stands 722 above Stan Musial, who won seven National League batting titles, and 641 above Albert Pujols.

Broken down, Aaron's 6,856 total bases would equal 1,714 home runs, 2,258 triples, or 3,328 doubles. A player would have to match Babe Ruth's single-season record of 457 and keep it up for fifteen years to even approach Aaron's record—and he'd still be one base short.

Not intimidated by any pitcher, Aaron hit a career-high 17 home runs against Don Drysdale and posted a .925 OPS against him—just three points shy of the slugger's .928 lifetime OPS.

He managed an .820 OPS or better against nine of the 13 Hall of Fame pitchers he faced at least 25 times. Two of his favorite targets were usually formidable left-handers Sandy Koufax (1.077 OPS against) and Steve Carlton (1.025 OPS).

A rare slugger who made good contact, Aaron had more walks (1,402) than strikeouts (1,383), never fanned 100 times in a season, and fanned far less often than Ernie Banks, Roberto Clemente, or Mickey Mantle.

He won batting crowns in 1956 and 1959, home run crowns in 1957, 1963, 1966, and 1967, and RBI titles in 1957, 1960, 1963, and 1966. He also led twice in hits, in 1956 and 1959.

Aaron and Mathews were teammates only at the ballpark, never in nightclubs. They liked and respected each other as ballplayers, with their different backgrounds only an issue when it came to carousing together after games. Aaron, mindful that a Black man partying with whites in bars could create issues, never joined Mathews and drinking buddies Warren Spahn, Lew Burdette, and Bob Buhl. Nor did he drink much anyway.

Aaron also avoided confrontation, while Mathews seemed to welcome it.

"Eddie was a big cat," Red Schoendienst once said of him. "You can pet him but don't try to corner him."

Mathews, good-natured when sober, was team captain of the Braves for years. He was respected by both teammates and rivals as a good competitor who would do anything to win. But he was like a walking volcano when drunk, likely to insult people of different races or religions. Aaron knew that but ignored it, instead trading playful insults with the lefty-hitting slugger.

The muscular third baseman wound up on the cover of the first *Sports Illustrated*, in 1954, and was tied with Willie Mays on the lifetime home run list, with 435, on the day Barry Bonds was born.

Aaron depended upon other teammates as well.

"When I was a rookie in 1954," he said, "we had Eddie Mathews and Joe Adcock, so I considered myself a guy who got on base. But when I got older and stronger, I also got more selective with the pitches I hit and that turned me into a home run hitter. Then it was my responsibility."

During the eight years Aaron and Adcock were teammates, the big first baseman actually averaged more home runs per at-bat than the outfielder.

Four of those came on July 31, 1954 at Brooklyn's Ebbets Field. He started a day-long rampage with a second-inning homer against Don Newcombe, then connected again in the fifth, seventh, and ninth, adding a third-inning double that gave him 18 total bases, a record at the time.

"I was a guess hitter," Adcock said, using a description often applied to Aaron. "Anybody who says he isn't just won't admit the truth. It's always better to be lucky than good."

Adcock finished with 10 grand slams, 28 multi-homer games, the homer-turned-double that ended the Harvey Haddix's perfect game, the first home run into the center-field bleachers of the Polo Grounds, and the first one that went over the grandstand at Ebbets Field.

When the Milwaukee Braves became the first team to hit four straight homers in a game on June 8, 1961, he hit one of them, joining Mathews, Aaron, and Frank Thomas.

At 6-foot-4 and 220 pounds, he looked like Paul Bunyan in a Braves jersey and had the back-of-the-card stats to prove it.

Neither Mathews, a Californian, nor Adcock, with Louisiana roots, gave Aaron any guff because of the color of his skin. Nor did Spahn, a native of Buffalo, New York, though the pitcher, also white, was guilty of some clubhouse teasing that bordered on the insensitive.

During his playing career, Aaron crossed paths with ten members of the Braves Hall of Fame. Four of them—Phil Niekro, Warren Spahn, Joe Torre, and Mathews—are also in the National Baseball Hall of Fame in Cooperstown. Braves Hall of Famers who played with Aaron were Adcock, Lew Burdette, Rico Carty, Del Crandall, Ralph Garr, and Ernie Johnson.

With 203 wins, a World Series MVP Award, and a no-hitter on his resume, Burdette is a borderline candidate for Cooperstown as well. A right-hander known for hijinks off the field and a well-hidden spitball that inflated his win total,

Burdette was Spahn's sidekick and the right-handed half of baseball's best 1-2 tandem for more than a decade. He also possessed some unknown ability to hit home runs against Sandy Koufax (three times!).

Crandall was the main Milwaukee catcher during Aaron's early years. A perennial All-Star who had considerable power for his position, his tenure with the team was ended by a trade that followed an injury—plus the emergence of Joe Torre.

Torre, who often caught Spahn and Burdette, came to the Braves as a favor to older brother Frank, the team's backup first baseman in the '50s. Once considered too fat to stay in the majors, he trimmed down to become a perennial All-Star and later, after leaving the Braves, a batting champion and MVP. Torre caught the first game in Atlanta, hitting the first two home runs in Atlanta Stadium, and later gave the team a 36-homer season. He also won a division crown as manager in 1982, albeit without Hank Aaron.

Niekro's claim to fame was a knuckleball nobody could catch. Called out of the bullpen for an impromptu start in 1967, he went on to win 318 games—most of them for the Braves—and help the team win divisional titles in 1969, with Aaron, and 1982, after he left. The soft-spoken Niekro was part of a brother tandem (with Joe) that won the most games (539) of any fraternal pair. He was one of 24 pitchers in baseball history in the 300 Club.

Carty and Niekro reached the Milwaukee Braves together, though the former made a much bigger splash. When he joined the Braves in 1964, Carty lived up to the "Beeg Boy" nickname he gave himself by challenging Richie Allen for National League Rookie of the Year honors. He later won a batting crown, became the game's first All-Star write-in, and fashioned a .317 average while wearing a Braves uniform. A former amateur boxer in his native Dominican Republic, Carty was such a defensive albatross that he needed to DH years before anyone knew what that meant. But he delivered an unforgettable hit to Hank Aaron's jaw during an airplane row that hastened his departure from Atlanta—not to mention from Aaron's room on road trips.

Dependability was not a Carty asset. He missed complete seasons in 1968 with tuberculosis and in 1971 with a fractured kneecap, suffered in the Dominican Winter League.

Garr, like Carty, won a batting crown while playing left field for the Braves. When he and Dusty Baker were rookie outfielders, Aaron took both of them under his wing, teaching them how to eat, dress, and behave as professional ballplayers—especially on the road. Garr, a little guy who could fly, was nicknamed the "Road Runner" because of his speed. He did not have Carty's power but did have a much calmer temperament—allowing him to forge a long post-playing career with the Braves as a scout, coach, and spring training base-running instructor.

Because he served as pitcher, publicist, and broadcaster for the Braves, Johnson became the only person to witness five different four-homer games in person: Gil Hodges in 1950, Adcock in 1954, Rocky Colavito in 1959, Willie Mays in 1961, and Bob Horner in 1986. A New Englander who started with the Boston Braves, Johnson was a relief pitcher before retreating to the safety of the broadcast booth.

Johnson, Skip Caray, and Pete Van Wieren broadcast Braves games for three decades on SuperStation TBS, founded by Turner after he bought the team. That same year, Turner made Bill Lucas, brother of Henry Aaron's first wife, the first black general manager. All five are members of the Braves Hall of Fame. Later general manager John Schuerholz, architect of the team that won a record 14 consecutive division titles from 1999–2005, was inducted into the Braves Hall of Fame in 2016 and the National Baseball Hall of Fame two years later. Technically, he was Hank Aaron's boss.

Bill Lucas, brother of Henry Aaron's first wife, was a well-spoken player who became the first Black general manager, while Schuerholz later served as the GM who put together the teams that won a record 14 consecutive division titles (1999–2005). Technically, he was Hank Aaron's boss.

Turner purchased the Braves in 1976 after Aaron left for Milwaukee. A savvy and innovative television magnate with a Clark Gable mustache and Bill Gates brain, he converted local station WCTG into the TBS SuperStation, beamed Braves games across the country, and saved a floundering franchise from finding greener pastures. After the 1996 Olympics, the Braves inherited the new Olympic Stadium and renamed it in his honor.

It was also that fall that Ted Turner brought Hank Aaron back to Atlanta after a two-year hiatus in Milwaukee. He would launch a new career as director of player development.

Hank Aaron's teammates also included future Hall of Famers Red Schoendienst and Orlando Cepada, who didn't spend enough time wih the Braves to make the team's Hall of Fame. At a Cooperstown event attended by Schoendienst in 1998, Eddie Mathews admitted, "We don't win the World Series that year [1957] if we hadn't got him."

The switch-hitting second baseman was acquired from the Cardinals just minutes before the trade deadline, helped the

Braves win consecutive pennants in 1957 and 1958, and then contracted tuberculosis that kept him sidelined for virtually all of the '59 campaign. Unable to plug the gaping hole at second base, the Braves slid into a first-place tie, then lost a best-of-three pennant playoff with the Dodgers.

Ten years later, the Braves also reached to the "Show Me State" for a star player. Cepeda arrived during a spring training trade for Torre, whose salary negotiations had gone sour. The National League's MVP just two years earlier, Cepeda proved a panacea for a season, playing a strong first base and adding considerable pop to the lineup of the '69 Braves team that won the first NL West flag. Though his chronic knee problems later curtailed his career, Cepeda still made it to Cooperstown.

Just as Schoendienst helped Aaron by reaching base in front of him, Cepeda helped by batting behind him—and forcing pitchers to feed him a steady diet of fastballs.

With Cepeda in the on-deck circle, Aaron had 44 homers and 97 RBIs in 147 games for the title team in that first year of divisional play. It was the first time since 1958 that Aaron reached the postseason, but the last time he ever got that far.

Two years later, Cepeda's chronic knee problems limited him to 14 homers in 71 games, opening the door for a freshman slugger named Earl Williams.

A Black corner infielder converted to catching in midseason by a pressing team need, Williams got through a difficult transition with Aaron's aid.

"When I first met Hank, he impressed me as a man with a lot of class," said Williams, who hit 33 homers en route to National League Rookie of the Year honors in 1971. "He carried himself well and was a quiet, soft-spoken guy.

"As the year went on, he more or less took me under his wing but it wasn't an active thing," said Williams, who hit 33 homers en route to NL Rookie of the Year honors. "He didn't just take me from the beginning of the year. It was a thing that grew gradually. It wasn't pushed on either part. I could come to him with questions and problems and he would help me."

Aaron's influence was most apparent in the success story of Dusty Baker, whose long career as a player and manager began with the Braves on a full-time basis in 1972. Baker, who spent eight seasons with the Braves before he was traded to the Dodgers, was an Aaron protégé even before he signed; the veteran slugger had promised Baker's mother he would take personal charge of her son, teaching him to how to dress, eat, and speak in a manner befitting a professional athlete.

Along with Garr, another promising Black player who broke into the lineup the year before, Aaron had a pair of apprentices. He would do for them what Bill Bruton had done for Aaron and other young Blacks on the Braves two decades earlier, when the team was still based in Milwaukee.

Since ballplayers see their teammates more often than their families during any given season, having a father figure in the clubhouse is a major factor in the development of young players—especially emotionally. Aaron's lessons, learned through his own hard experience, included tips on talking to teammates, coaches, fans, and especially members of the media.

With those lessons in mind, Baker went on to win World Series rings as both a player and a manager. He guided five different teams into the playoffs and, at seventy-three years of age, became the oldest manager to win a World Series when his 2022 Houston Astros defeated the Philadelphia Phillies.

A lock for a future niche in Cooperstown, Baker is not yet in the Braves Hall of Fame—an oversight that needs to be corrected. Darrell Evans, Aaron's Atlanta teammate from 1969–1974, should also be considered.

"His 713th home run was also his 40th home run of the 1973 season," Evans said. "He told reporters how proud he was to be part of the first 40-homer trio in baseball history and even took Davey Johnson and me to the press conference with him. That meant so much to us.

"I was a young player (twenty-six) at the time but the longer I played, the more I appreciated the little things that were going on. The thrill of going through that with him was unmatched.

"I will always remember April 8, 1974. There was never a more important sports moment in my lifetime."

CHAPTER 11

BROTHERLY LOVE

Baseball history is filled with brother tandems.

There were five Delahantys, headed by Hall of Famer Ed, at the turn of the twentieth century, and four O'Neills, led by veteran manager Steve O'Neill.

There were three DiMaggios: Joe, Vince, and Dom.

There were three Alous: Felipe, Matty, and Jesus.

There were plenty of pairs, too, from the Alomars (Roberto and Sandy Jr.) and the Bretts (George and Ken) to the Walkers (Dixie and Harry) and the Waners (Paul and Lloyd), the latter the only brother tandem in the Baseball Hall of Fame.

Among brother combinations, the three Alous played the most games, the Waners combined for the most hits, and the DiMaggios had the most RBIs.

Fourteen members of the Hall of Fame actually had brothers who lasted at least 10 years in the major leagues: Roberto Alomar, George Brett, Ed Delahanty, Joe DiMaggio (twice), Rick Ferrell, Tony Gwynn, Greg Maddux, Pedro Martinez, Phil Niekro, Gaylord Perry, Cal Ripken Jr., Joe Sewell, Lloyd Waner, and Paul Waner.

There were brother batteries, brothers in the same double-play combinations, pitching brothers who won 20 games in the same season, and pitching brothers who both won 200 games.

The Waners homered in the same game three times and same inning twice. On September 15, 1938, they went back-to-back—a feat duplicated by Melvin and Justin Upton of the Atlanta Braves, also in the fifth inning, on April 23, 2013.

No other brother tandem has ever hit consecutive home runs. But several did it in the same inning at least twice—with the Uptons and Ripkens (Cal Jr. and Bill) joining the Waners and Aarons on that exclusive list.

The Aarons? Tommie has become little more than footnote in baseball history, but had his moments in the sun.

If anything, Tommie was hurt by his own surname. When he reached the majors in 1962, eight years after his older brother, everybody expected him to continue the Aaron dominance.

"With me around, it was difficult for Tommie to be his own ballplayer," Hank admitted.

Branded a utilityman because he could play multiple positions, Tommie never got the fair shake his minor-league record demanded. During a career that lasted seven seasons, he played six positions—all three bases and the three outfield positions—but was used most often at first base, where he was a good if not gifted fielder.

He finished with a puny total of 13 home runs, two of them walk-offs.

Hank and Tommie homered in the same game three times and in the same inning once—on July 12, 1962.

The Milwaukee Braves, playing at home against the St. Louis Cardinals, fell behind in the first inning and stayed there until the last. Then the Aaron brothers took over.

With one man out and nobody on, Tommie came up to pinch-hit for pitcher Claude Raymond and connected on a pitch from Larry Jackson, then the top St. Louis starter. The ball disappeared into the left-center field bleachers at County Stadium.

With the Cards still leading by a 6–4 score, leadoff man Roy McMillan singled—sending Jackson to the showers.

Normally reliable closer Lindy McDaniel—who had not yielded an earned run since May 31—allowed a single to Mack Jones, then walked Eddie Mathews to load the bases with one out. As a result, McDaniel faced the next-to-impossible task of coaxing a ground ball from Hank Aaron.

Though dealing with a painful ankle, Henry relied on his quick wrists. He hit a 2-1 fastball over the fence for his third grand-slam of the season, and the only game-ending grand slam of his career. Milwaukee won the game, 8–6, and the *St. Louis Post-Dispatch* reported that both Aarons homered to almost the same spot in the ballpark.

Ironically, it was long-time Cardinals lefty Curt Simmons who said, "Trying to sneak a fastball by Hank Aaron is like trying to sneak the sun past a rooster."

During his 23-year career, Hank Aaron would end nine games with home runs, including the blast that won the 1957 National League pennant five years earlier, but only on that occasion would one of his walk-offs come with the bases full.

It was the first time since 1938, when the Waners did it, that brothers teamed up to produce such timely long balls.

In addition to the constant comparisons to his superstar brother, Tommie fought a constant battle of the bulge.

"I've talked to him about his hitting," Hank once said, "but you can't tell a fellow how to hit. I tell him what I know about certain pitchers, things like that. But I've talked to him more about his weight. That's been his biggest problem. He has to watch his weight."

Hank was a solid 6-footer who weighed 180 pounds and rarely deviated, eating carefully and keeping trim through a variety of physical activities, including tennis, racquetball, and swimming. Tommie stood 6-foot-3, tipping the scales at 190 or more, but looked chunkier. He lacked his brother's quick, powerful wrists and speed on the basepaths.

In addition to the scales, Tommie also had to watch the daily transactions sheet. As a player, he had more ups and downs than the Empire State Building elevator.

After signing on May 28, 1958, at age eighteen, Tommie played for the Braves in both Milwaukee (1962–63 and 1965) and Atlanta (1968–1971), but also played so well when given regular work in the minors that he won International League MVP honors in 1967. That brought the well-liked Mobile native back to the majors after a three-year absence.

He hit .250 in 1969 but batted only 60 times. "It seemed like they never gave me a chance," Tommie confided. "But not everyone can be Hank Aaron. That guy's unique in the world. He's the complete ballplayer who can do just about anything. I had to scuffle."

That fall, Hank and Tommie became the first fraternal pair to play together in the postseason as the Braves faced the "Miracle" New York Mets in the first National League Championship Series. Although Hank homered three times, the Braves fell fast, losing three straight in the best-of-five series, which sent the winner to the World Series.

Two years later, on September 24, 1971, Tommie played his last game, leaving the playing ranks with a .229 lifetime average,

216 hits, 13 home runs, 94 RBIs, and 102 runs scored in 437 games.

Less than three years passed before Hank Aaron became baseball's new home run king.

"The day he breaks the record," Tommie said in 1973, "I'll feel just as happy as he will—probably happier. Look, he's my brother. I love him. I keep watching the papers and anytime he hits a home run, I feel great."

Like his brother before him, Tommie tuned up for the majors at Eau Claire, Wisconsin, where he hit 26 home runs in 1959. The following season he hit 20 for Cedar Rapids, based in Iowa.

Signed for the Braves by John Mullen, the same man who brought Hank Aaron to the organization from the Negro Leagues, Tommie hit right-handed—the same as his brother.

In 1961, after hitting .299 for a Double-A team in Austin, Texas, he joined the Braves as the understudy to veteran first baseman Joe Adcock. He got a hit in his first game—a single against future Hall of Famer Juan Marichal. By then, the Aarons were not only teammates but roommates.

"He impressed me as a good hitter," boasted his beaming brother, who also became Tommie's roommate on the road. "He doesn't fall away from the plate. He hangs right in there."

That was evident when he batted leadoff in a May 25 game against the Cardinals; Tommie's four hits included doubles against Curt Simmons, Bobby Shantz, and McDaniel.

On May 30, the Aarons combined to beat the Reds. Tommie singled against Dave Sisler in the ninth, moved to second on a sacrifice, and scored on a single by Henry.

In another Milwaukee home game, against the Los Angeles Dodgers on June 12, Hank and Tommie homered in the same game for the first of three times. Hank connected with the bases empty in the second against Phil Ortega while Tommie cracked a two-run shot against Ed Roebuck in the eighth. The Braves won handily, 15–2.

It was such a laugher that manager Birdie Tebbetts had Lee Maye pinch-hit for Hank in the home seventh. A partisan crowd of 10,376, displeased that the Braves were mired in sixth place, 14 games behind the Dodgers, was not amused. They were more distressed a night later when Sandy Koufax hit the first home run of his career to beat Warren Spahn, 2–1.

A month later, when the Aarons double-teamed the Cardinals, the Milwaukee faithful were rewarded.

Tommie continued to shine in August, where he filled in at first base for the injured Adcock. The younger Aaron hit .333, posted a .423 on-base percentage, and had 28 hits and 13 walks in 27 games.

One of those hits, on August 4, was a game-ending grand slam against Phillies closer Jack Baldschun that gave the Braves a 7–3 victory and Tommie as many game-winning slams as his older brother.

Also in August, the Aarons homered in the same game for the third and final time. Against the Reds at Crosley Field on August 14, Tommie tagged Johnny Klippstein in the sixth and Hank homered an inning later against Ted Wills. Milwaukee won, 5–4.

Tommie finished the '62 campaign with 20 doubles, eight home runs, and a .231 batting average in 141 games. It was the best season of his career.

But it wasn't his last hurrah as a player. In a 1965 exhibition game against the Detroit Tigers, Tommie hit the first home run in Atlanta Stadium, the new circular ballpark built to lure the Milwaukee Braves south.

After the team transferred from Milwaukee to Atlanta in 1966, Tommie became a minor-league manager and later a major-league coach. At thirty-three, when it became obvious that his talents lay more in coaching than playing, Tommie became the first Black manager in the southeast when the Braves installed him as pilot of their farm team in Savannah.

"I'm really pleased for him," Hank said after Tommie was selected to manage Savannah. "He has a good baseball mind and I think he'll be a good manager. I just hope the people won't get the idea that the Braves gave him the job because of me. That's not the way it was. Tommie earned it on his own and he'll hold it on his own."

He managed Dale Murphy and other future stars in the minors, then coached under Bobby Cox and Joe Torre in Atlanta.

Together, the Aarons hit 768 home runs, more than any brother combination in baseball history. Tommie was the first brother of a 500 Home Run Club member to even play in the majors, although Eddie Murray's brother Rich later did likewise.

Had he not lost his life to leukemia on August 16, 1984, Tommie Aaron was on track to realize an ambition his older brother once harbored: to manage in the major leagues.

Although Frank Robinson became the first Black manager in the big leagues when the Cleveland Indians hired him in 1975, Hank Aaron had indicated his own interest in becoming a manager or executive a season or two sooner, as his playing days neared an end.

Tommie Aaron's No. 23 has been retired by the Gwinnett Stripers, who succeeded the Richmond Braves as Atlanta's

Triple-A affiliate. Before the International League franchise moved, it also established the Tommie Aaron Memorial Award, given to the team's Most Valuable Player each year.

Tommie himself never won an MVP as a major-league player, but was the Most Valuable Person for many who knew him, including his brother.

Hank Aaron, at Tommie's bedside when he passed, said that experience was "the hardest night of my life."

CHAPTER 12
MANAGERS MAJOR AND MINOR

During a professional career that spanned more than two decades, Henry Aaron played for managers of many temperaments and abilities. Most were former players, some former teammates, and one became a member of the National Baseball Hall of Fame before Aaron also landed there.

The only thing they had in common was that all were white—with the exception of Buster Haywood, a Negro Leagues veteran who managed the teenaged Aaron for three months with the touring Indianapolis Clowns.

"I never really cared who the manager was," Aaron once said. "I mean it doesn't bother me personally. I wanted a manager who was going to be good for the team as a whole but as far as I'm concerned, the manager wasn't important to me—as a personality.

"The manager wasn't going to change the way I played. I owed it to myself and my family and the fans who believe in me to play as well as I could play at all times, no matter who the manager was."

But managers, like bosses in any occupation, invariably inspired better performance when they were popular and lesser results when they weren't.

Not infrequently, players have said of managers, "I would run through a brick wall for him."

Aaron's first minor-league manager was Bill Adair, a fellow Mobile native who ran the Eau Claire team in the Northern League. For Aaron, an eighteen-year-old Black kid who had never been away from home, the biggest challenge was not facing unfamiliar pitchers but living in a situation that, for him, seemed light-years from home. He called his mother often, told her he was quitting, and was always talked out of it by brother Herbert.

Adair managed just 10 games in the majors, on an interim basis with the 1970 White Sox, but was a finalist for several jobs. He eventually coached in the majors a dozen years later when Birdie Tebbetts was skipper for the Braves. That was fine with Aaron, who said at the time, "He was a lot more than a manager to me. I think because he was a Southerner he was even a little more understanding of the little Black kid he had playing beside him."

Throughout his career, Aaron insisted that his favorite manager was Ben Geraghty, a Villanova product who played sparingly for the Brooklyn Dodgers and Boston Braves during the war years but found his niche as a minor-league manager. He had 1,432 wins, a .554 winning percentage, and five pennants in seven years in the Braves farm system. From 1953–1962, none of his teams finished lower than second.

Aaron was just nineteen when he encountered Geraghty in Jacksonville, then a Double-A affiliate of the newly relocated Milwaukee Braves.

Faced with the triple whammy of a segregated city, a room-mate (Felix Mantilla) whose English was limited, and a manager who didn't hesitate to correct his mistakes, the soft-spoken Aaron succeeded by letting his bat speak for him.

He led Jacksonville to the Southern League pennant by hitting .362 with 36 doubles, 14 triples, 22 home runs, 115 runs scored, and 125 RBIs—a performance that produced an MVP Award.

Also that season, the budding slugger was inspired by Barbara Lucas, whose brother Bill would later become general manager of the Atlanta Braves. They were married by the time Aaron reported to Caguas of the Puerto Rican Winter League.

Mickey Owen, the manager there, was also influential in Aaron's early years. Realizing his potential, Owen moved Aaron from the middle infield to the outfield, where he didn't have to worry as much about his defense.

Owen also tinkered with Aaron's batting stance and hands placement but took a hands-off approach about the prospect's habit of hitting off his front foot—the result of a boyhood injury to his right ankle. The manager must have made the right decision: after a slow start, the kid took the batting title with a .357 average.

A former catcher whose 13-year career was tarnished by a World Series passed ball that turned the tide of the 1941 Fall Classic from the Dodgers to the Yankees, Owen—like Geraghty—let Aaron play his way, boosting his confidence.

But jumping from the Sally League or the sultry Caribbean to the cauldron of major-league baseball was like jumping from one side of a smoldering volcano to the other.

The Milwaukee Braves were stacked, with Andy Pafko, Billy Bruton, and Bobby Thomson in the outfield (from right to left),

Johnny Logan at short, Eddie Mathews and Joe Adcock at the infield corners, and newly acquired Danny O'Connell at second.

For Aaron, all signs pointed to Toledo, then the top Milwaukee farm club.

But that was before young Henry stepped into the batter's box.

Veteran manager Charlie Grimm, who went with the Braves from Boston to Milwaukee when the franchise moved during 1953 spring training, had seen glowing scouting reports on Aaron but had never seen his face, his swing, or his power potential. Nor had he ever seen a ballplayer like Hank Aaron.

The unorthodox batting stance and quick wrists were not the only novelties; the whole approach of the young wunderkind looked like he was in dreamworld. Totally relaxed but confident at the plate, Aaron would later be accused of falling asleep between pitches.

His running and fielding had similar hallmarks. He would move with grace, conserving his speed unless he absolutely needed it to reach a ball or take an extra base.

The manager began referring to him as "Stepin Fetchit," after Black Vaudeville star Lincoln Theordore Perry, who often portrayed a wandering minstrel. It was not intended to be a racial slur but as a tribute to the first Black star of the American cinema.

Grimm, whose baseball career began with the Philadelphia Athletics in 1916, was thrilled with Aaron's hitting potential but not enamored by his defense at either shortstop, his original position, or second base. The advance scouting reports—and the eyewitness reports from special spring training instructor Paul "Big Poison" Waner and fellow Hall of Famer Ty Cobb—came to the same conclusion.

"As a second baseman," Grimm mused, "Aaron is a very good hitter. But we'll find a place for that bat."

Not even on the official roster, Aaron needed only one thing: a break. He got exactly that, on March 13, 1954. In a game at Al Lang Field in St. Petersburg, Thomson suffered a triple fracture of his right ankle after an awkward slide into second base. Initial estimates of his absence were six to twelve weeks.

The next day, the cleanup spot in the Braves' lineup read, "Aaron, RF." And so it would remain for most of the next twenty-three years.

One day before the opener, the Braves promoted the twenty-year-old. He played left field in his first game, with Pafko shifting to right.

By season's end, young Henry had a solid .280 batting average, 13 home runs, and pins in his ankle—the result of a fracture suffered while sliding into third base, on September 5. That cost the young-and-hungry team a possible pennant and cost Henry the Rookie of the Year Award once won by Jackie Robinson. The trophy went instead to Wally Moon, with Ernie Banks and Gene Conley also getting more votes than the young Aaron.

Without Aaron, Milwaukee finished third, eight games behind the front-running Giants and three behind the Dodgers.

Grimm, one of the last managers to serve as his own third-base coach, had won three pennants in 19 seasons as a major-league manager. But the outgoing, guitar-playing pilot was considered too close to his players and not enough of a disciplinarian. Although the Dodgers and Giants were formidable foes in the eight-team National League, the Milwaukee Braves never finished higher than second under Jolly Cholly.

On June 27, 1956, with the Braves off to a sluggish start with a 24–22 record, Fred Haney was hired to replace Grimm—even though his three-year record with the team was solid. Grimm's Braves went 92–62 in 1953, 89–65 in 1954, and 85–69 in 1955, finishing second twice and third once.

Haney, who had managed bad ballclubs with the St. Louis Browns and Pittsburgh Pirates, finally had the horses to win—and he did.

Recharged by the managerial change, the Braves went 68–40, a .630 winning percentage, and held a one-game lead over the Brooklyn Dodgers entering the final weekend. But Milwaukee lost two out of three to St. Louis while the Dodgers swept the Pirates to clinch the flag.

Haney told his frustrated players he would emphasize fundamentals in spring training. "You're going to hate my guts next spring," he said, "but you'll love me when you see that World Series check in the fall."

He was right—thanks in part to an MVP season by Aaron and a matching Cy Young campaign by Warren Spahn.

Unlike Grimm, Haney kept his players at arm's length. He also annoyed them by chewing them out in front of their teammates during clubhouse meetings. In addition, Haney alienated Aaron by tinkering with his batting order, often batting Aaron second rather than third or fourth—the traditional RBI spots.

The manager's theory was that batting Aaron second would gain him more at-bats, and thus more home run opportunities, but the player thought it would reduce his ability to knock in runs. It wasn't until early June that the manager restored the slugger to his usual clean-up spot in the order.

It was the same month that the Braves made the trade that turned them into world champions, sending Bobby Thomson and Danny O'Connell to the St. Louis Cardinals for second baseman Red Schoendienst, a nine-time All-Star who instantly solidified the position in Milwaukee.

Later in the season, Haney got more help when a twenty-seven-year-old outfielder named Bob Hazle burst onto the big-league scene as an injury replacement for center fielder Bill Bruton, who had injured his knee in a collision with shortstop Johnny Logan.

Hazle hit so well, so hard, and so unexpectedly that he soon took on the nickname "Hurricane" after a storm that wreaked havoc along the East Coast the previous fall. The twenty-seven-year-old rookie hit .493 in August and .403 in the 41 games he played for the Braves before he, like a hurricane, dissipated and disappeared. In the meantime, Aaron replaced Bruton in center, creating space in the lineup for Hazle more than half-a-century before the designated hitter became universal.

Aaron wasn't thrilled but accepted the assignment, though he slipped to .255 in August after establishing himself as a Triple Crown contender earlier in the campaign. He would revive in September, eventually hitting the pennant-clinching home run against Billy Muffett of the St. Louis Cardinals.

For the 5-foot-5 Haney, by far the shortest manager in the majors, the entire 1957 season was a matter of survival.

Haney was a frequent target of the Milwaukee press and was also blamed by author/analyst Bill James for blowing pennants in both 1956 and 1959. The indictment included platooning Joe Adcock with the weaker hitting Frank Torre; over-reliance on Spahn and sidekick Lew Burdette; ignoring promising pitchers

Joey Jay and Juan Pizarro, who became stars elsewhere after ill-advised trades; and turning his bench into an Over the Hill Gang with Enos Slaughter, Mickey Vernon, Bobby Avila, and other non-contributors.

James said the '59 Braves should have finished 20 games ahead of the Dodgers and called Haney's performance the worst example of managing in baseball history. According to James, the Braves could have easily won four pennants in a row and started their own mini-dynasty.

Instead, the Dodgers seized the opportunity after the Braves abdicated.

Had the manager been Leo Durocher instead of Fred Haney, that probably wouldn't have happened. Rumors persisted for years that Braves ownership was infatuated with Durocher, who won pennants with the New York Giants in 1951 and 1954, but the marriage was never consummated.

Even Aaron, during his MVP season, ran afoul of Haney— not only because of their initial kerfuffle about the slugger's slot in the lineup but also because of an incident that occurred during a game. Aaron banged into a double play with two men on and was so disgusted with himself that he waltzed down the first-base line.

The next day, in a team meeting, Haney said, "Henry, you mean a lot to this team and everybody else is trying to win a pennant. You didn't look like you cared yesterday and I want you to know that, by God, I *do* care. You didn't hustle on that double-play ball. You loafed.

"Of course it was a double play but suppose somebody had kicked the ball. What chance would you have had if you were jogging along halfway down the baseline? None. You might have stopped a rally. We won the game but that makes no difference to me. You loafed."

That was the end of it, for both men. Haney hung on, despite such hair-brained tactics as starting Carlton Willey in the opener of the best-of-three pennant playoff against the Dodgers in 1959, and the Braves continued to win, though not quite enough to conquer the relentless Dodgers.

He wound up as the most successful manager in the 13-year lifespan of the Milwaukee Braves, the only team in baseball history that never had a losing season. Haney's Braves won 341 and lost 231, good for a .596 winning percentage. He still had a losing record as a manager, however, since the Browns and Pirates proved to be perennial losers. Overall, Haney was 626–797 for a .454 percentage.

Without Hank Aaron, it would have been far worse.

"When he left the Braves," Aaron said, "I hated to see him go and the older players hated to see him go. I thought he was a good manager."

The next man to sit in the Milwaukee manager's seat was Chuck Dressen, who had led the Brooklyn Dodgers to consecutive pennants from 1951–1953, but blew a 13.5 game lead capped by Bobby Thomson's "shot heard 'round the world" in his first year at the helm. An outspoken egotist who once told the National League All-Stars that he'd use the signs he'd stolen from their teams during the season, Dressen was so confident that one writer predicted he'd finish three games ahead of his own ballclub.

In 1960, Aaron earned all of $45,000—a pittance considering his consistent excellence but all he could squeeze out of tight-fisted general manager John Quinn in the days before agents, unions, and free agency. Still, it was a lot better than the $6,000 he had earned as a rookie six years earlier.

Not one to let money interfere with performance, Aaron knocked in 121 runs and collected 334 total bases, both league highs, as Dressen's Braves finished second, seven games behind the surprising Pittsburgh Pirates of Dick Groat and Roberto Clemente.

When they dropped to fourth in 1961, however, Dressen was out and Birdie Tebbetts was in. Tebbetts, like Dressen, had started his managerial career in Cincinnati.

A former catcher who inherited an aging team, Tebbetts did not have a good relationship with Warren Spahn, Lew Burdette, or Eddie Mathews, all of whom were on the downsides of their careers. Switching to a five-man starting rotation upset Spahn, whose streak of six straight 20-win seasons ended as a result. A workhorse used to making relief outings between starts, Spahn still won 18 games but worked four games less than he had the year prior.

Even though 1962 marked the first expansion of the National League, which went from the old eight-team format to ten, the Braves could not take advantage. They even lost a double-header to the hapless New York Mets at the Polo Grounds in May en route to a fifth-place finish, 15 games behind the first-place Dodgers.

When they dropped to sixth a year later, 15 games behind, Tebbetts saw the handwriting on the wall. He wrote two letters, which he left on his desk for his successor.

Bobby Bragan, a former Brooklyn infielder who had previously managed Pittsburgh, found the letters when he arrived in 1963. The envelope on the first letter read, "Open when you get into trouble." A few weeks later, with the team still struggling, Bragan opened the second one. It read, "Prepare two letters."

Bragan was a protégé of Hall of Fame executive Branch Rickey, who hired him as an unproven thirty-year-old manager at Fort Worth in 1948—one year after Jackie Robinson integrated the game.

Robinson's arrival had caused a crisis of conscience for Bragan, who joined a group of teammates in signing a petition against adding him to the team. He was so adamant that he even asked Rickey to trade him. But Bragan changed his mind after the first road trip and told Rickey he was honored to be Robinson's teammate. "Branch Rickey made me a better man," Bragan said at the time. He also earned Rickey's trust, became a coach, manager, and eventually president of the Southern League—the same circuit that Aaron helped integrate in 1953.

Once thrown out of a game for offering the home-plate umpire a drink of orange juice, Bragan was an impatient type who was willing to try anything to ignite his team. He tried iron-fisted outfielder Rico Carty as a catcher and let his starting pitchers work so deep into games that Spahn threw an estimated 200 pitches during a 1–0, 16-inning loss at San Francisco on July 2, 1963. But he also moved Aaron from fourth to third in the lineup, reasoning that he'd always come to bat in the first inning—and perhaps put the team ahead with a home run.

The move must have worked, since the 1963 season might have been Aaron's best. He not only finished first in home runs, hits, total bases, and runs batted in but also enjoyed the only 30/30 campaign of his career.

Bragan, a brash but innovative manager, reasoned that the most effective batting order should have the usual No. 3 hitter first, the No. 4 hitter second, and the normal leadoff and No. 2 hitters at the bottom. His theory was that the best hitters on the team would thus get some 50 more at-bats than they otherwise would.

After he went south with the team in 1966, Bragan tested his idea, making Felipe Alou the leadoff man. The Braves led the league in runs scored, thanks to a personal-peak 31 home runs from Alou, who also had a league-best 218 hits. But the pitching was so poor that the team lost too many games and cost Bragan his job.

Billy Hitchcock, a Bragan coach and yet another Alabama native, replaced Bragan on August 8, 1967, and immediately reversed Bragan's policy of platooning the left-handed Mathews, whose prolific power had begun to fade. The next night, with Sandy Koufax throwing bullets at the Braves in Atlanta, Mathews beat Koufax with a solo home run in the bottom of the ninth. The team, including Aaron, celebrated as if it had won the World Series.

Hitchcock was also the man who made a starter out of an unknown knuckleball reliever named Phil Niekro. Given a start when Ken Johnson took ill, Niekro blanked Philadelphia and went on to post the best ERA (1.87) of his career and, years later, to join the exclusive 300 Club.

Unfortunately for Hitchcock, he never had the pitching to sustain a race for the pennant. As a result, he became the only one of Aaron's managers who never had a full season in the job.

Sticking with their Alabama theme, the Braves next turned to Lum Harris, a former World War II Navy veteran who pitched for the Philadelphia Athletics before and after his wartime combat service. A long-time friend of Paul Richards, his batterymate with the 1938 Atlanta Crackers, Harris worked for Richards with the Chicago White Sox, Baltimore Orioles, and Houston Colt .45s before joining the Braves as a minor-league manager, major-league coach, and eventually major-league manager.

In his second year at the helm, 1969, Harris led the Braves to an unexpected first-place finish in the new National League West—the first year of divisional play, where the National League somehow decided Atlanta and Cincinnati when "western" teams while Chicago and St. Louis wound up in the east.

The peculiar alignment created a postseason pennant playoff between the Braves and upstart New York Mets, a young, pitching-powered team that caught fire down the stretch. The Braves won 93 games but lost three straight to the upstart "miracle" Mets despite three home runs from Hank Aaron.

The good times didn't last. When the team's fortunes fell over the next few years, both Richards and Harris lost their jobs.

That enabled Mathews to become the first man to play for, coach for, and manage the Atlanta Braves. He was also the first man to play for the Braves in each of their three home cities, Boston, Milwaukee, and Atlanta.

A combative competitor who never shied away from a fight or a bottle, Mathews had to manage himself as well as his team. From Aaron's perspective, however, Mathews acquitted himself well, shielding his old friend from the incessant demands of the media, protecting his privacy as much as possible, and taking the blame from baseball commissioner Bowie Kuhn when a controversy erupted over Aaron's playing time in the three-game Cincinnati series that would open the 1974 season (mentioned earlier in this book).

Although Mathews tinkered with his lineup throughout the season, he always batted Aaron fourth, where virtually every manager (except Bragan) thought he could help the team most. Even when Aaron slipped into a long funk after his historic home run, he still hit cleanup.

During the time they were teammates, Mathews and Aaron hit more home runs than any other tandem. Both were headed to the Baseball Hall of Fame. But Mathews couldn't hang on and was released when the Braves slipped to 15 games behind—even though they had a winning record at 50–49. Aaron and third baseman Darrell Evans, to whom Mathews had been a mentor, both condemned the decision.

Clyde King, a Southern gentleman and teetotaler whose laidback personality proved a stark contrast to Mathews, took over on July 23, 1974. Responding to the change like a breath of fresh air, the team went 38–25 to reach 88 wins—its best performance since 1969.

Like Bragan, King had Rickey roots; he not only pitched for Brooklyn when Rickey was running the ballclub but was on the 1947 team when Jackie Robinson reached the majors. That earned him extra respect from Hank Aaron.

At the end of the season, however, Aaron was traded to Milwaukee—the same city where he had started his career. The Brewers were managed by another old colleague, Del Crandall.

A young team that gravitated to Aaron even though his talents were waning with his age, the teenaged Robin Yount and other young players gathered in the outfield to have conversations with Aaron about baseball, professionalism, and life in general. It was a Fireside Chat without the fire. And it was Crandall's idea—even though he knew from his Milwaukee days that Henry Aaron was not exactly loquacious.

Once the season started, however, the good memories of spring wilted like an unwatered flower. Against a bevy of unfamiliar pitchers, Aaron's average sagged to embarrassing depths. The slugger himself, who had been hitting third mostly out of respect to his past accomplishments, asked Crandall to drop him lower in the batting order.

The Brewers proved to be a bust, costing Crandall his job, and the forty-two-year-old Aaron had to deal with another new manager in what would prove to be his final season.

He considered retiring but remembered he had a two-year contract that called for $240,000, good money at the time.

"I thought I could earn it," he said somewhat wistfully. For once, Aaron was wrong.

Playing just 85 games, he hit .229 with 10 homers—none after July 20. That shot, against Dick Drago of the California Angels, was the 755th of his career.

Used exclusively as a designated hitter by the Brewers, Aaron added 22 American League home runs to his National League count of 733. An outfielder at heart, the old man still shagged flies and worked out in the outfield before games but it was simply a matter of pride—and a way of setting an example for the young players on the team.

No better under Grammas than they were under Crandall, the Brewers went 68–94 in 1975 and 66–95 in 1976.

It was not until 1982, with Harvey Kuenn as manager, that the Milwaukee Brewers reached the World Series for the only time in their history. Long before then, Hank Aaron had returned to Atlanta as an executive in the front office of Ted Turner's Braves.

HOME RUN KING

Hank Aaron's Managers			
Seasons	**Manager**	**Team**	**Record**
1954–56	Charlie Grimm	Milwaukee Braves	198–156 (.559)
1956–59	Fred Haney	Milwaukee Braves	341–231–3 (.590)
1960–61	Chuck Dressen	Milwaukee Braves	159–124–1 (.560)
1961–62	Birdie Tebbetts	Milwaukee Braves	98–89 (.524)
1963–66	Bobby Bragan	Milwaukee/Atlanta Braves	310–287–2 (.518)
1966–67	Billy Hitchcock	Atlanta Braves	110–100 (.524)
1968–72	Lum Harris	Atlanta Braves	379–373–2 (.503)
1972–74	Eddie Mathews	Atlanta Braves	149–161–1 (.479)
1974–75	Clyde King	Atlanta Braves	96–101–1 (.485)
1975	Del Crandall	Milwaukee Brewers	271–338 (.445)
1976	Alex Grammas	Milwaukee Brewers	66–95 (.410)

CHAPTER 13

FAMILY MAN

Although he came from a large family and produced one of his own, Henry Louis Aaron's life off the field resulted in a roller coaster of emotions not unlike the ups and downs of a pennant race.

He had two marriages while also dealing with the deaths of parents, siblings, and even children throughout his baseball career.

His father, Herbert, who spent thirty years working in the segregated Mobile docks as a ship fitter's helper and eventually a welder, made $900 a year—not enough for his wife Estella to buy meat or for young Henry to afford baseball equipment.

It was a big deal when Hank signed with the semi-pro Prichett Athletics for $2 a game. He later got a "raise," to $3 a game, with the Mobile Black Bears, another semi-pro outfit. In both cases, the teenaged Aaron was the youngest and smallest man on the field—or close to it. But his talent superseded his size.

Young Henry took odd jobs to bring in more money. Both he and his father even picked cotton at various times, possibly thinking they were still on a plantation during the dark days of slavery.

Segregation was bad enough—and persisted years after the US Supreme Court struck it down.

Regardless of the Jim Crow laws in Alabama and other Southern states that once comprised the Confederacy, survival of the family was paramount.

When Henry made $200 a month with a $2 per diem for food money in his first baseball venture, he sent $125 back to his mother in Mobile and subsisted on peanut butter sandwiches. "There was no jelly because we couldn't afford it," he later said.

Before Henry parlayed his baseball ability into a decent and regular paycheck, his family often couldn't afford meat. They consumed whatever they could grow. "I ate a lot of vegetables," Aaron remembered.

Things gradually got better for young Henry and his family.

But then they got worse.

"One of my sons passed away as an infant," he said, "and my first marriage was rough. My divorce was really something to go through, especially with four kids involved. I threw myself into baseball to get my mind off it but there were still periods when I was really depressed. It took a long time to get back on the right track.

"I was struggling to get over the divorce at the same time I was starting to close in on the home run record. The Ruth chase should have been the greatest period of my life, but it turned out to be the worst."

Aaron was a nineteen-year-old minor-leaguer when he married Barbara Lucas while playing in Jacksonville in 1953. During their eighteen-year union, they produced five children: Gary, Lary, Dorinda, Gaile, and Hank, Jr. But the family suffered the tragic loss of Gary, one of the premature boys born on December 15, 1957, along with Lary.

The Aarons had a comfortable home in a Milwaukee suburb—far from the segregated South—and were not happy when the team pulled up stakes. Henry had bitter memories of his childhood in Alabama and even worse memories of Jacksonville, when fans openly taunted the three Black players forced to integrate the all-white Sally League while white teammates made no secret about harboring similar sentiments—as if Aaron were Jackie Robinson with the 1947 Brooklyn Dodgers.

Barbara was vocal about her opposition to Atlanta, causing a rift in her marriage that never healed. It was difficult for Henry, who came from a large family and now had one of his own.

An altercation between Barbara and ballpark security forces on July 30, 1966, didn't help. It was the team's first season in Atlanta. When she tried to drive into the family parking lot, Mrs. Aaron was not recognized or allowed entry. She protested, police were called, and three officers were suspended.

Two years after his divorce from Barbara, Henry married Billye Suber Williams on November 13, 1973, and adopted the widow's daughter, Ceci. They also adopted the Catholic religion after meeting a Milwaukee priest, Father Michael Sablica.

"He taught me what life was all about," said Aaron. "But he was more than just a religious friend of mine, he was a friend because he talked as if he were not a priest sometimes."

They played golf together and even talked religion, especially after Father Mike found a book called *The Life of Christ* in Aaron's car. The book later found its way into the player's clubhouse locker.

Among other things, the cleric convinced Aaron to become more vocal about civil rights issues and to attend Mass every Sunday. That was hard in Bradenton, the Florida spring training home of the Milwaukee Braves, because even the churches were segregated.

"Hank is a very unusual human being," the priest said at the time. "He has a naturally good mind and you can't help sensing that his consciousness has evolved to a high level. His mental and physical preparation for a game is remarkable."

That preparation included playing handball, swimming, fishing, and reading.

Henry met Billye, an Atlanta television host, when she was assigned to interview several Braves in 1971. "I was only dimly aware of his existence or even of the Braves at that time," she said. "And I had never seen the team play."

Twice before his appearance, Aaron had cancelled.

Married two years later, Billye soon became a ballpark regular, cheering and screaming with other Braves fans. "You should see the way we jump up and down when Hank gets a homer," said Carla Koplin, the secretary assigned to handle Aaron's mail and other matters. "She's very cool otherwise but then she shouts and yells as we hug each other."

Like her fiancé, Billye felt the pressure of the Ruth race.

"It's like living in a fishbowl," she said late in the '73 season. "I'm pleased he's finally getting the recognition he deserves but people are fickle. Today's fans may be gone tomorrow. Since Henry's not the flamboyant type, I don't think breaking the record will generate as much attention as it might have."

Billye got plenty of attention herself, hosting the popular Atlanta television show *Today in Georgia* and carrying on the work of her first husband, Dr. Samuel Williams, co-founder of the Southern Christian Leadership Conference and one-time mentor of Dr. Martin Luther King Jr.

"Samuel was very much in the public eye," said Billye. "He was always being quoted in the papers and I was involved in fund-raising work with him."

Almost the second she married Henry, Billye found herself thrust into an even bigger and brighter spotlight. But she relished their private moments.

"He's a fantastic person and a fun guy although he doesn't come on to be because he appears very serious all the time," she said late in the '73 season. "And yet he has a way of breaking out of that shell."

Aaron enjoyed his family time.

"I'm quite close with my kids," he said between marriages. "The oldest boy wants to play football. He's pretty close to his coach and his teammates. I want him to get into things he wants to get into—rather than doing things simply because he's Hank Aaron's son."

When Aaron's daughter Gaile was twenty—the same age he was when he broke into the big leagues—she described her father in an emotional article for the student newspaper at Fisk University, where she was a journalism major.

"In my estimation," she wrote, "Hank Aaron is not a two-legged home run machine. He is a mild-mannered, concerned person with human interests, giving great concern for his four children—Hank Jr., Lary, Dorinda, and myself—their education and their future. During his 20-year career, Daddy has received many gifts, trophies, and proclamations, but I still feel his most cherished gift is Dorinda, presented to him eleven years ago on his birthday.

"As I sit in the stands and hear the fans applaud for Mr. Brave, it makes me feel good to know that this is my father they love."

Gaile later made headlines with a syndicated story about her father and the pressures he faced. Part of that story explained the family's feelings.

"Hank Aaron is under tremendous pressure," she wrote, "but even we as a family can't really detect it. I guess it's because of his keen sense of humor.

"There is a different Hank Aaron than the one the world knows. In my opinion, he is the greatest in baseball but he could most definitely use some pointers on telling jokes—well maybe on the punch lines.

"Nevertheless, he manages to cheer you up regardless of the situation. On the other hand, he is a man of his word. Soft-spoken he may be but if the point is to be gotten across, you get it loud and clear. I can never remember him spanking a great deal. He has this approach he uses, with a soft tone of voice that will tear your heart out without even touching you.

"As an ending note, I would like to express the importance of Babe Ruth's record not only to my father and his family but also to Black people and the youngsters of America. It is not every day that something like this takes place in a person's lifetime.

"This achievement is being accomplished by a Black man. This points out to the youth of America that if effort is put forth and patience is insured, accomplishments are possible, keeping in mind that time is an important factor. After all, this is the first time in forty years this record has been challenged."

Years later, Gaile told biographer Howard Bryant that Hank was a better father than a baseball player. "I was always, 'Gaile

Aaron, Hank Aaron's daughter' but it wasn't good enough to be just Gaile," she said.

A humble hero, Aaron told his children that neither he nor they were better than anyone else.

"He just had a job that was in the limelight," Lary said. "He always said he's no better than a guy digging a ditch."

All five Aaron children went to college. "My father wanted me to go to college," said Henry, whose mother wanted him to become a teacher. "Sometimes I wonder what my life might have been like if I couldn't play ball."

Aaron's parents, so prominent the night he broke Babe Ruth's record, lived to see their son become the home run king. Estella, his mother, lived to age ninety-six, while dad Herbert Sr. made it to eighty-nine. Like any proud parents, they tried to save every clipping they could find about their famous son.

Those clippings, plus various medals and trophies Aaron won over the years, were still located in the den of his boyhood home when the City of Mobile, Baseball Hall of Fame, and Aaron himself kept it alive as a baseball museum adjacent to Hank Aaron Stadium, home of the Mobile Black Bears semi-pro team that Henry once used as his springboard to stardom.

The house, built by patriarch Herbert Aaron Sr. in 1942, took an eight-mile trip by flatbed truck on October 30, 2018, with Mobile architect Larry Hinkle footing the $50,000 moving cost. Since the enterprise was designed as a 75th birthday present to Henry, both of his parents and five of his eight siblings were long gone. But they were there in spirit.

So were Hank's children, from Gaile, his oldest, to Dorinda, his youngest.

Lary Aaron, who played football for Florida A&M before his ill-fated attempt to play professional baseball, became a physical education teacher and part-time scout for the Milwaukee Brewers. But he never forgot where he was when his father broke Babe Ruth's record.

"We watched the game at my grandmother's house in Jacksonville, Florida," he said. "We weren't able to be there because we all got death threats. But we were able to call him and talk to him on the phone right after the broke the record."

Before Henry completed his run around the bases, two fans evaded security and ran up to the outfielder between second and third. "We were kind of scared when we saw them," Lary remembered of the teenaged fans, who spent that night in jail but later became physicians. "But they ended up writing books, too. And my dad became good friends with them."

An outfielder who played a little first base, Lary said his famous father, then farm director of the Braves, insisted he get his education. "My dad was more about education than he was about sports," he said. "He told me to go back, get my degree, and have something to fall back on. That's what I did. I taught school in Milwaukee, then moved to Atlanta and worked there.

"My dad had a foundation that sent a lot of kids to college who couldn't afford it."

Behind the scenes, Lary Aaron gave hitting lessons to Michael Harris II, an Atlanta native who became a star center fielder for the Braves. He was also aware of the threatening messages received by his father.

"My dad never brought his business home," Lary said, "so we never knew about the death threats until the beginning of the 1974 season. He saved more than five hundred of those letters."

As for the nine voters who left Hank Aaron's name off their 10-man Hall of Fame ballots for the Class of 1982, Lary had a one-word explanation: "Racism."

The girls made good, too. Dorinda, the youngest child from Henry's first marriage, worked in advertising before joining her father's 755 Restaurant Corporation, an umbrella organization that included Krispy Kreme donuts, Church's Chicken, and Popeye's franchises. Cecile Aaron Haydel, born to Henry and Billye, became a professor at Morehouse, where the Aarons donated considerable scholarship money.

When Ceci's daughter Emily Haydel got her bachelor's degree in sports management from the University of Michigan in 2017, Henry made it a point to attend. "This means more to me than when I hit 715," he told a local reporter.

"I'm so happy for Emily, her mom, and her grandma. When I went to see her as a tiny tot in the hospital, I was hoping I would live long enough to see her march down the aisle at her graduation."

It was Emily's dad Victor Haydel to whom Aaron sold most of the fast-food franchises he once owned. Among them were a handful of Krispy Kremes, famous for their HOT DONUTS signs, and nearly two dozen Popeye's.

"I tell young people—including my granddaughter—that there's no shortcut in life," Aaron said during a rare interview with the *Detroit Free Press*. "You have to take it one step at a time and work hard. And you have to give back."

Hank Aaron, Jr.—called Hankie by the family—later threw out the first pitch at a Truist Park tribute to his father.

"Sometimes I think I should have named him anything but Hank Jr.," his father once said. "It might be too much of a burden on him and that would be very unfair."

Just having the Aaron surname definitely hurt Tommie Aaron, the only Aaron sibling who also played professional baseball.

"He never had the opportunity to prove what he could do with the club," Henry said of his younger brother. "The Braves never played him enough. I know he could have been a very good ballplayer if he'd signed up with somebody other than the Braves."

Like Bill Lucas, brother of Barbara Aaron, Tommie's life ended prematurely.

Lucas, hired by Ted Turner as the first Black general manager in baseball history, suffered a cerebral hemorrhage and died at forty-three in 1979. Tommie died of leukemia five years later at age forty-five—short-circuiting his bid to become one of the first Black managers in the game.

Tommie had been Hank's teammate and roommate when the pair played together with the Braves in both Milwaukee and Atlanta. Hank was in his fifth season when the team, still based in Wisconsin, signed Tommie on May 28, 1958.

Their personalities came from opposite poles, with Tommie the talkative, outgoing type and Henry the Quiet Man. But the younger brother had the gift of gab plus the sense of humor that touched the heart and soul of his introverted but famous sibling. He made Hank laugh, though Tommie's constant trips up and down between the majors and minors were no laughing matter to the brothers. They hated their separations.

Their other siblings included sisters Sarah, Gloria, and Alfredia and brothers James and Herbert Jr. Another brother, Alfred, died of pneumonia at an early age.

Henry outlived sisters Sarah, who died of diabetes at seventy-one, and Gloria Delilah Robinson, a teacher who died in

2004; brother Herbert Jr., who passed away in 2002; as well as Tommie and his parents. The year 1998 was especially tough: both his father Herbert Sr. and oldest sister Sarah passed within two months of each other.

At his father's funeral, Henry said in his eulogy, "He was poor and unlearned yet he was rich and wise. You might say he had a Ph.D. in common sense. He did his share of bragging about me. Now I'm bragging about him."

Stella survived ten more years, moving in with the Aarons in Atlanta as her age and medical issues worsened.

Alfredia Aaron, an advertising executive, married politician David Scott in 1969 and eventually emulated her athletic sibling by donating thousands of dollars in scholarships to needy Black students. Her husband was first elected to represent Georgia's 13th Congressional District in 2003.

During his final season as an active player with the Atlanta Braves, Hank Aaron told a writer he wanted to become a full-time father. Left implied was the fact that he had done virtually everything anyone can do between the white lines of a baseball diamond.

"I want to see my kids grow up," said Aaron, whose oldest child in 1974 was twenty-year-old daughter Gaile, then a journalism major at Fisk University in Nashville.

He did, hitting his best and longest home run as a fulfilled family man.

CHAPTER 14

COOPERSTOWN

It took a while, but Hank Aaron finally got the recognition he deserved from the National Baseball Hall of Fame.

The "Chasing the Dream" exhibit, which dominates the museum's second floor, is all things Hank Aaron—from his humble beginnings in Mobile semi-pro ball to his worldwide acclaim as a record-breaking athlete and respected humanitarian.

It is also one of only two Cooperstown exhibits devoted to a single player. Not surprisingly, the other salutes Babe Ruth.

"He was always a fan favorite in Cooperstown," said long-time Hall of Fame president Jeff Idelson. "His legacy was national, not regional.

"Henry loved being inside the Hall of Fame. He was very proud of it and loved being in that setting."

Even after he slipped on rare ice in front of his Atlanta home, he still came to Cooperstown five months later, though leaning on wife Billye and a cane.

At the dawn of the twenty-first century, Aaron decided to donate all his memorabilia to the museum, Idelson said. "He believed what we did was supportive of him, the Negro Leagues, baseball in general, and the game's role in elevating society.

"I went to Atlanta with a couple of colleagues and cataloged everything he had. After his mom passed away, we took his childhood home, put it on a flatbed truck, and turned it into a living history museum.

"Once that happened, Tom Seaver, who worshipped Henry, said, 'If Henry is doing it, I'm doing it.' Ichiro said the same thing. Four Black high schools came out to honor him and left an empty rocking chair on the porch as a salute to Henry."

Idelson, now sixty, is a Boston native who watched Aaron conclude his career with the Milwaukee Brewers. "I was very fortunate I was getting the chance to see a legend," said Idelson, who went to Fenway Park with his father for those games against the Red Sox.

"In my heart, Hank Aaron is the home run king," he insisted. "Barry Bonds is the home run leader only because Major League Baseball allowed it to happen.

"Henry is still the all-time leader in runs batted in, extra-base hits, and total bases. Take away all his home runs and he still has more than 3,000 hits."

Idelson marveled at Aaron's personality.

"Low-key guys are hard to figure out," he said. "Henry wasn't the quintessential showman but succeeded without having to be showy. I don't think I ever met anyone as consistent as he was, especially considering his demeanor off the field. He was even-keeled and that helped him a great deal."

Aaron's legacy would have been so much larger had he played in a media capital, Idelson said. Instead, the slugger was overlooked because he played in Atlanta before the advent of Ted

Turner's TBS SuperStation and, prior to that, in the much smaller market of Milwaukee.

"What the home run chase of 1998 did was allow the lens on Henry to become even wider," said Idelson, who served as public relations director of the Yankees before moving to Cooperstown. "The way he felt about civil rights, the City of Atlanta, his care for the game, and humanity were all taken to a new level."

Aaron and his artifacts were the centerpiece of a gallery of records called "One for the Books," which became "Chasing the Dream" following a special ceremony in 2010.

"The friendship I developed with him over time is still unfathomable to me," Idelson explained. "I'd be sitting around on a Saturday afternoon, and he'd call to say, 'Are you watching the Falcons game?' He'd ask my opinion about guys. He had his own opinions but was quiet about them. He really cared about people, especially his fellow Hall of Famers.

"We loved our relationship with him as a museum. And his love was so profound that he donated everything. It was a great love-love relationship."

For visitors to the Hall of Fame, it's impossible to bypass the sprawling Aaron exhibit, which includes such artifacts as the bat, ball, and uniform he used when breaking Ruth's home run record in Atlanta on April 8, 1974.

Also included are the bats and balls from Aaron's 3,000th hit, 500th and 600th home runs, and even the last one, his 755th, hit while playing for the Milwaukee Brewers in 1976.

So are his 1957 World Series ring and National League Most Valuable Player trophy, both the only ones he won during his 23-year career; the Medal of Freedom presented to him by

President George W. Bush in 2002; and enlarged quotations from Mickey Mantle and Muhammad Ali.

"As far as I'm concerned," Mantle said in 1970, "Henry Aaron is the best baseball player of my era."

Ali must have approved, since his quote reads, "Hank Aaron is the only man I idolize more than myself."

Not all of the writers who voted for Hall of Fame candidates in the cold winter of 1982 agreed. Nine of them—nine!—decided to omit the lifetime home run leader from their 10-name ballots.

That deprived Aaron of his wish to become the first unanimous inductee and suggested that the malignant tumor of racism that had dogged the slugger throughout his career had shrunken only slightly.

With 97.8 percent, Henry Aaron ranked second at the time to Ty Cobb's 98.2 percent in 1936, when the first Hall of Fame class was selected. The percentage was also higher than anyone—including his idol Jackie Robinson—received since the end of the color line in 1947.

"I'd be lying if I said I didn't want to be unanimous," Aaron told writer Howard Bryant, author of *The Last Hero*, "but I realize nobody has been. I'm happy with the number of votes I received."

With 406 of 415 ballots cast, the quiet man from Mobile not only finished ahead of Willie Mays, Mickey and the Duke (Duke Snyder), but also ahead of Babe Ruth, the legend whose shadow seemed to follow Aaron everywhere.

Another shadow Aaron had sought to escape was cast by the 6-foot-5-inch commissioner of baseball, Bowie Kuhn.

There was no congratulatory telegram after his 700th home run, no personal appearance on the night of his 715th, but plenty of interference in 1974 after the team announced it wanted Aaron to hit the historic home run at home—and not in the Braves' opening three-game series in Cincinnati.

Now it was eight years later and tempers had cooled, though maybe not memories. After touring the Hall of Fame with his family on Friday, July 30, Aaron had breakfast with Kuhn Saturday, discussed their differences, and settled matters on the Otesaga Hotel's tennis court. The younger, more athletic Aaron won.

The next morning, Aaron filled the nervous hours before his induction with a friendlier tennis match, against former teammate Frank Torre. As soon as they were finished, Aaron showered, dressed, and polished up his induction speech.

His audience that afternoon would include his parents, Estelle and Herbert Aaron, and wife Billye, as well as their five children, several siblings, and numerous baseball colleagues, including Kuhn, the two league presidents, Braves owner Ted Turner, and an All-Star roster of former teammates.

More comfortable facing a Sandy Koufax fastball than any listening audience, an emotional Aaron gathered his thoughts, then said, "I feel especially proud to be standing here where some years ago Jackie Robinson and Roy Campanella paved the way and made it possible for Frank [Robinson] and me and for other Blacks hopeful in baseball. They proved to the world that a man's ability is limited only by his lack of opportunity."

The Class of 1982 included not only Aaron and Robinson but former baseball commissioner Happy Chandler and New York Giants shortstop Travis Jackson.

"Twenty-three years ago," Aaron said in his speech, "I never dreamed that this high honor would come to me. For it was not fame I sought but rather to be the best baseball player that I could possibly be. I grew up in a home where there was little in the way of material goods. But there was an abundance of love and discipline."

Before thanking those in attendance, as well as his admirers in Atlanta and Milwaukee, Aaron added, "The sheer majesty of this occasion and its significance overwhelms me. For truly I reflect on my life and particularly on my twenty-three years in baseball. I am reminded of a statement I once read and I quote, 'The way to fame is like the way to heaven. Through much tribulation.'"

His trials and tribulation extended beyond the bigotry he endured, first as a Black man and secondly as a Black man who dared to challenge records long held by white men. There were also perceived slights suffered at the hands of writers voting for postseason awards and even by the Hall of Fame, where Aaron's name was not always prominent and items he donated were not always displayed properly—if at all.

He also bristled when he saw the statues of Babe Ruth and Ted Williams—two white men—greeting visitors to the Hall of Fame Gallery, where plaques of the greats are posted in perpetuity.

The hurt remained even after Aaron was informed that the museum displays only 10 percent of the items in its vast and rotating collection at any given time. But the sting lessened after he saw his first pro contract, an old locker donated by the Braves, and photographs taken some thirty years earlier. All are part of "Chasing the Dream," a rare exhibit with permanent status.

Although there was a significant gap in Aaron's attendance at the annual midsummer inductions, he returned for the wave of Braves who dominated the ceremonies from 2014–2018, with seven men selected over five years.

Even after he fell on unexpected black ice outside his Atlanta home in February of 2014, Aaron felt well enough to come to Cooperstown on a cane to witness the inductions of Bobby Cox, Tom Glavine, Greg Maddux, and Joe Torre in 2014. He was back a year later for John Smoltz, then in later years for Chipper Jones and John Schuerholz.

When introduced to the vast crowd outside Clark Sports Center, where induction ceremonies were held during those years, he invariably got the loudest and longest standing ovations of anyone on the star-studded dais.

That made his day—and made the difficult trip to Central New York well worth the trouble for an old man with a long memory.

CHAPTER 15
QUOTEBOOK

"Hank Aaron is the best ballplayer of my era. He is to baseball of the last fifteen years what Joe DiMaggio was before him. And you know what? Nobody would recognize him if he walked through that door this minute. It's tragic. He never received the credit he's due."

—Mickey Mantle

Bartlett's Familiar Quotations was a mere drop in the ocean compared to the myriad of quotes by and about Henry Louis Aaron.

About Hank Aaron

The most famous was a line widely attributed to St. Louis Cardinals southpaw Curt Simmons, who gave Aaron considerable trouble with his variety of slow curveballs and changeups:

"Trying to sneak a fastball by Hank Aaron is like trying to sneak the sun past a rooster."

That was true even in 1954, when Aaron was a svelte rookie trying to make a big impression.

Admiring the large red 41 on the back of Eddie Mathews, Aaron asked traveling secretary Donald Davidson if he could trade in the No. 5 he wore that year for a jersey with double numerals. No. 44 was not taken, but Davidson wasn't quick to let it go.

"You're too skinny to carry the weight of two big numbers on your back," he told Aaron before giving in.

Not long after that, Aaron faced a young Brooklyn lefty named Sandy Koufax. "Hank was the toughest out I ever faced," Koufax admitted. "I remember one game in 1955 against the Braves in Milwaukee. Hank came up the first time and got a single. The next time up he hit a home run. The third time, he slid into second with a double. I remember walking near the base and I called over to him and said, kiddingly, 'Mr. Aaron, next time you come up I'm going to throw my shoe at you. See how far you can hit that one!"

Despite his difficulties with Aaron, Koufax was a bonus baby who blossomed into a Hall of Fame starter after taking the roster spot of fellow southpaw Tommy Lasorda. Pittsburgh reliever Roy Face had better luck with Aaron—perhaps because he faced him for shorter stints.

"If it wasn't for me," Face said, "Henry Aaron would only have 754 home runs. I'm proud to say Henry hit only one home run off me over the years. It was in my final year in the big leagues when I was in Montreal with the Expos in 1969. It was a great way for him to say, 'Goodbye and good luck,' I suppose."

The Godfather of home runs, Aaron delivered that Kiss of Death greeting to hundreds of pitchers, none so noteworthy as those who delivered the gopher balls that tied and broke Babe Ruth's record in 1974.

After Jack Billingham yielded Aaron's 714th home run, allowing him to tie Babe Ruth's record, he said, "It wasn't a bad pitch, but it wasn't good enough against Hank Aaron."

Four days later, Al Downing threw the pitch that turned into the record breaker and said, "I never say 7:15 anymore. I now say, 'quarter after seven.'"

Bespectacled left-handed reliever Tom House caught the ball in the Braves bullpen, then raced toward home plate with the prize. "It was a really cool moment for me," he said. "I caught the ball . . . *the* ball! I realized if I didn't catch it, it would have hit me in the head. I gave the ball to Henry while he was being hugged by his mother. There were tears in his eyes. It was one of those moments in life you never forget."

Like House, who never amounted to much as a player, former teammate Bob Uecker was a big part of Aaron's life. "We were good friends for a long time," said Uecker, who became a Brewers broadcaster as well as a Johnny Carson regular. "Henry used to love those spots when I was on the *Tonight Show* over the years, especially how I would talk about all the fantastic things I didn't do and make them sound really good. Like how it was really special to have two hits in one season."

Not only did Uecker and Aaron have adjacent clubhouse lockers but even did humorous commercial spots for Magnavox in Milwaukee. "It took thirty minutes to do a thirty-second spot," Uecker said. "All we did was laugh."

Longtime teammate Phil Niekro, whose march toward Cooperstown began after the Braves obtained Uecker to catch his knuckleball, watched Aaron for years but never pitched against him.

"I couldn't even pitch against him during batting practice in spring training," said Niekro, who took most of his 318 lifetime wins with the Braves. "He wouldn't let me because of the knuck-leball. When I went out there, I always wanted to throw a few knuckleballs in batting practice and get the feel for the batter and the strike zone. Henry didn't want me to do that."

Ralph Garr, along with Dusty Baker, were Aaron's surrogate sons when they reached Atlanta in the early seventies. "He told us to be a good teammate and respect the game of baseball," said Garr, a former batting champion. "He wasn't a guy who made a whole lot of noise or said a lot. But if you ever went to him for advice, he would really take pride in giving you the best advice he thought possible for that situation."

Without Aaron looming in the lineup behind him, Garr said, he would not have won the 1974 National League batting title. "He's one of the most beautiful people in the world and you have no idea how many people he's helped," he said at the time. "As great a ballplayer as he was, he was even a better person."

Baker, who later took five teams into the playoffs as a man-ager, stayed close with Aaron long after both retired as players. "We were playing in Atlanta when I was managing the Reds," Baker said, "and one day Hank came to visit me in the manager's office. I had told my players all about Hank, so when Joey Votto and Jay Bruce saw Hank, they asked me to introduce them. All they wanted to do was just meet and talk with Hank and they did. They were like two little kids."

Another Atlanta mainstay, two-time National League MVP Dale Murphy, was one of many stars whose big-league careers began after Aaron became Atlanta's director of player develop-ment. He too had high praise for the home run king.

"It's been the honor of a lifetime to be able to wear the same uniform Hank Aaron wore," said Murphy, who won consecutive trophies in 1982–1983. "Hank's spirit permeated our whole organization. If you wanted to be a ballplayer, this is the way you play. If you want to represent your organization, this is how you act. If you want to serve your fellow man, this is what you do."

A later Braves slugger who won an MVP, Chipper Jones said of Aaron, "He's the greatest player I've ever laid eyes on and in the top two or three of the greatest human beings I've ever come in contact with. He just had this peaceful ease about him. I don't know where it came from or how he attained it.

"He was the epitome of confidence in the box. His mentality was, 'If you throw it over these 17 inches and I got you timed up, I'm going to hit this ball 450 feet and there's nothing you can do about it.'"

John Schuerholz, architect of the Braves teams that won a record 14 consecutive division titles, was Atlanta general manager when Aaron was director of player development.

"Technically, I was his boss because I was the GM of the organization," Schuerholz said during the 2023 Hall of Fame Induction Weekend. "But I don't think anyone ever felt they were the boss of Hank Aaron. He was a star player beyond measure, a star human being beyond measure.

"He was a great player—one of the greatest to ever put on a uniform in our game. But after that, he was somebody who liked to come down the hallway and talk to people like myself and others, see what was going on, find out how everybody was going, and that's what he did.

"I was talking baseball with George Brett, and he was telling me how aggravated he was with all the strikeouts in baseball now. That reminded me of Hank Aaron. They had the same attitude.

People just strike out. They don't hit balls. They don't put balls in play. They don't do anything."

Aaron had the respect of rivals too—even strikeout king Nolan Ryan.

"He was always an extremely tough out because he didn't chase bad pitches," said Ryan, a major-leaguer for a record 27 seasons. "He was very disciplined, very conscious of the strike zone. He also hit the ball where it was pitched. I remember he hit two home runs off me—one in each league. He also broke up a no-hitter of mine, I think in the eighth inning, when he was with the Milwaukee Brewers."

Catcher-turned-manager Jeff Torborg remembered, "There was no one way to get him out. He was quick as lightning. You couldn't put the ball in the same spot over and over; he would get to it. If you wanted to get him out with a fastball, you had to get him way out and away or up and in. If you made a perfect pitch, you *might* get him."

When Torborg was catching for the Dodgers, Aaron fouled a slider off his ring finger. "It knocked my finger straight up in the air," Torborg said. "The old umpire Jocko Conlan pulled it and straightened it out. The pitch was practically by him, but he got a piece of it and a piece of me."

Hall of Fame first baseman Willie McCovey respected Aaron too. "I think everyone has always known that Hank was special except for Hank," he said. "He was just so modest. But he was a hero to all of us. Hank was my favorite player. I wore 44 in honor of him."

According to Chicago Cubs star second baseman Ryne Sandberg, "Hank is one of the first names I think of when I think about the greatest players who have ever played the game.

I can't even imagine what he must have gone through and he was one of the greatest the game has ever seen. To do what he did despite all of those obstacles was just incredible. If I were to name five guys on one hand whom I consider to be the best, Hank Aaron would be No. 1 or No. 2."

Another second baseman enshrined in Cooperstown, Jerry Coleman faced Aaron in the 1957 World Series. "I am being very sincere when I say he was the most legitimate home run champion of all time," said Coleman, who later became a big-league broadcaster.

Walter Alston, whose career as manager of the Dodgers began the year Aaron was a rookie with the Braves, had some regrets. "More than anyone else," he said, "Hank Aaron made me wish I wasn't a manager. I know there just isn't any way to pitch to him."

Sparky Anderson, who also earned a Hall of Fame plaque as a manager, obviously felt the same way; he ordered Aaron intentionally walked with two outs and a man on third. "I'm not going to let Hank Aaron beat me in that situation," said the pilot of The Big Red Machine. "I wouldn't care if he had retired and come down out of the stands to hit. He lives for those situations."

As Aaron approached Ruth's record in 1972, his advancing athletic age did not dissuade Gene Mauch, then managing the Montreal Expos, from approaching him with extreme care.

"Two years ago, I didn't think he was going to do it," Mauch said. "He had ailments, like his knee, that were not publicized at the time. But apparently he got it under control and if he can average 120 games the next three years, he'll make it.

"I'll tell you this: we still feel the same about him as we did fifteen years ago. Any pitch above the belt is next door to disaster."

Pitcher Bill Lee agreed. "I was mad at Hank for deciding to play one more season," the lefty said. "I threw him his last home run and thought I'd be remembered forever. Now I'll have to throw him another."

Jim "Mudcat" Grant was so impressed by the home run king that he told his great-grandchildren Aaron once hired him as a minor-league pitching coach. "What Hank Aaron has done for the game is unbelievable," said Grant, who pitched for seven different teams. "I have always marveled at the player Hank was. He will always be part of baseball history and is so far up there in terms of his accomplishments on and off the field.

"He is a very smart man because he hired me to be a pitching coach. When I told my great-grandchildren, they said, 'Poppy, who is Hank Aaron?' I got the opportunity to tell them stories of that great man. Sometimes I worry because his accomplishments are so silent around the game because of Hank's quiet demeanor and because he wasn't flashy. Yet he faced as many problems as Jackie and many of the early Black ballplayers."

Don Money, who played against Aaron in Philadelphia but with him in Milwaukee, found him eager to share information. "My first year in the majors was at short, so when he'd be on second, I found him not at all reluctant to talk between pitches with a rookie," Money remembered. "What impressed me most at the time was Henry's friendliness. After spending a season with him, I know my first impressions were true. It became very easy to talk with him and develop a relationship that felt warm and comfortable."

Bobby Bonds, father of Barry, was the right-fielder for the Angels when Aaron hit his 755th and final home run. "My dad used to talk about Hank and Willie all the time and just what they meant to the game. I love being associated with him. He's such a classy and gracious man."

Mays, the rival slugger who almost became his teammate twice when the New York Giants and Boston Braves were engaged in a bidding war for Negro League stars, took notice of Aaron.

After the Atlanta star collected his 600th home run against San Francisco star Gaylord Perry at Atlanta-Fulton County Stadium early in the 1971 campaign, Mays said of Aaron, "He's not through rocking this place yet. If you think fans got shook up tonight, tell 'em to just stick around."

Even today, fifty years after he broke Ruth's record and three years after he died, the Aaron influence in Atlanta is pervasive.

"Our brand and our team are who we are because of Hank Aaron," said Derek Schiller, Braves president and CEO. "I know there are a lot of guys who have worn the uniform but none like Hank."

Baseball commissioner Rob Manfred called Aaron "an agent of change in our society" when he spoke at his Truist Park memorial service weeks before the start of 2021 spring training.

"Just as Jackie Robinson was the perfect person to change our game forever in 1947," he said, "Hank Aaron was the perfect person to meet the historic moment that he created in 1974."

By Hank Aaron

Quiet, taciturn, and sometimes stoic to the outside world, Hank Aaron did not turn out quotes like Yogi Berra or Satchel Paige.

The world didn't know it, but Aaron was a funny guy. Modest and humble to a fault with the media, he liked to laugh in the clubhouse, razzing teammates with good-natured banter.

Backup catcher Paul Casanova, who formed a strong friendship with Aaron, remembered one incident in Montreal: "We'd lost eight in a row and Hank came to bat in the ninth inning with two men on and us down by two runs. He hit one that was headed way out of the park. Everybody in the dugout jumped up and started screaming because our losing streak was about to end. But the wind caught it and brought it back into the ballpark, where the left fielder caught it at the fence. On the bus to the airport, nobody said anything for thirty minutes. We felt terrible. Finally, Hank stood up in the back of the bus and said, 'I'll bet any amount of money that damn Babe Ruth was up there blowing it back.' It loosened everybody up and we started playing better ball after that."

Minutes after breaking Ruth's record in 1974, Aaron trotted out to his position in left field when he realized that traveling secretary Donald Davidson was running after him, arms waving frantically. The winded Davidson blurted out that President Nixon was on the phone. "Well fine, Donald," Aaron said, "but what would you want me to do? Stop the game? I told him to put the President on hold and I'd be right with him."

Quick with a quip, Aaron once answered a reporter's question by saying, "Does Pete Rose hustle? Before the All-Star Game, he came into the clubhouse and took off his shoes and they ran another mile without him."

Aaron's even temperament helped him; beyond putting up with a barrage of abuse from loud-mouthed drunks in the stands and letter writers who hid behind the cloak of anonymity, Aaron never ran afoul of umpires. Not once was he thrown out of a game.

"Things do bother me," he admitted, "but I react differently than other people. Some guys go 0-for-4 and throw their helmets or kick things. But I think, 'Why did I pop up? Why did I strike out?' I'm never satisfied, really. I always feel there's room for improvement."

That was certainly true of Aaron's golf game.

"It took me seventeen years to get 3,000 hits in baseball," he said, "but I did that in one afternoon on the golf course."

As a wide-eyed rookie outfielder in 1954, Aaron still had a lot to learn. "I made some silly mistakes as a kid with the old Milwaukee Braves," he said twenty years later, "but I played on such a great club that they were overlooked."

Accepting failure is part of the job, Aaron noted.

"Everybody who is successful has failed sometime," he once said. "That's one of the beautiful lessons of baseball. It doesn't matter how great a hitter you are. Two of every three times, you're going to fail. A lot of people never understand that it's all right to fail as long as you make the attempt."

He spoke about Ruth's record, though not necessarily by choice.

"Babe Ruth will always be No. 1," he said. "Before I broke his record, it was the greatest of all. Then I broke it and suddenly the greatest record was Joe DiMaggio's hitting streak.

"Records are made to be broken. You make records and people try to break them. No matter whether it's Barry Bonds, Mark McGwire, or anybody else, records are going to be broken."

Roger Maris broke Ruth's single-season record with 61 in 1961. "Roger lost his hair the season he hit 61," Aaron said as he also approached Ruth. "I still have my hair but when it's over, I'm going home to Mobile and fish for a long time."

His home run record stood for thirty-three years.

"I don't want them to forget Babe Ruth," he said of the fans. "I just want them to remember Hank Aaron."

The media certainly remembered, though Aaron himself said he didn't pay much attention to statistics. "That's something for the men with the pencils to worry about," he told a gaggle of reporters in Atlanta. "I'll hit as many homers as I can, and you guys figure out what it comes to."

Aaron created a name for himself with consistent excellence in all phases of the game.

"I realize that if I hadn't been able to hit the hell out of a baseball, I would have never been able to lay a finger on the good life I've been fortunate to have," he said. "Playing baseball has given me all that a man could ask for—certainly a lot more than a timid little Black kid like me ever dared to dream about."

Of his twenty-one years with the Braves, he said, "I came to the Braves on business and I intended to see that business was good as long as I could. Consistency is what counts; you had to be able to do things over and over again.

"There was no backup plan. It was baseball or nothing. It had to work."

He never watched any of his 755 home runs. "I've never watched any of my home runs," he said early in 1974, when his home runs became historic. "I let the umpires do that."

A paragon of patience at the plate, Aaron explained his approach.

"Patience is something you pick up pretty naturally when you grow up Black in the state of Alabama," he said. "When you wait all your life for respect and equality and a seat in the front of the bus, it's nothing to wait a little while for a slider inside."

Aaron knew Black players had to be especially good. "There's only one way to break the color line," he said years after Jackie Robinson broke it. "Be good. I mean *play* good. Play *so* good that they can't remember what color you were before the season started."

Although Jackie Robinson was his inspiration, Joe DiMaggio was his role model.

"When he played," said Aaron of the Hall of Fame center fielder, "he always threw to the right base. He ran, he caught the ball. He did all the right things. He was an idol of mine in the outfield. He played the game the way it was supposed to be played."

Like DiMaggio, Aaron took the game seriously.

"I never smiled when I had a bat in my hands," he said. "That's when you've got to be serious. Nothing was a joke to me when I got out on the field. I didn't feel I should walk around with a smile on my face. And looking at the ball going over the fence wasn't going to help."

The epitome of confidence, Aaron said he feared no pitcher.

"I never worried about the fastball," he said. "They couldn't throw it past me, none of them. There wasn't any pitcher I couldn't hit. I looked for the same pitch my whole career: a breaking ball.

"When you're hitting, all pitches look alike. I didn't care too much who was throwing and what he was throwing. I liked those lefties but when my timing was off, I had trouble. When it wasn't, I didn't."

To Aaron, advance preparation was essential—even though he was a confirmed guess hitter.

"I started getting ready for every game the moment I woke up," he said. "I used to play every pitcher in my mind before I ever went to the ballpark.

"So many hitters do not know how to get themselves prepared to play or hit against a pitcher. You have to be mentally prepared to hit against all pitchers. Guessing what the pitcher is going to throw is 80 percent of being a successful hitter. The other 20 percent is just execution."

The key to longevity, Aaron always insisted, was desire. "Making the majors is not as hard as staying there, staying interested day after day. It's like being married. The hardest part is to stay married."

Good players are good because they can overcome all sorts of obstacles, from slumps to nagging injuries on the field or personal problems away from the park.

"My motto was always to keep swinging," Aaron revealed. "Whether I was in a slump, feeling badly, or having trouble off the field, the only thing to do was to keep swinging. What separates a superstar from the average ballplayer is that he concentrates just a little bit longer.

"If I knew exactly what I know now and had to do it over, I'd be a switch-hitter. No telling what I could have done."

In his return to Milwaukee as designated hitter for the Brewers in 1975, he started slowly, eventually connecting for his first American League home run. "I was happy to hit one out," he said. "I had to practice my trot."

About his approach at the plate, Aaron said, "The pitcher has only got a ball. I've got a bat. So the percentage in weapons is in my favor and I let the fellow with the ball do the fretting.

"The thing I like about baseball is that it's one-on-one. You stand up there alone and if you make a mistake, it's your mistake. If you hit a home run, it's your home run.

"Home runs win a lot of games but I never understood why fans are so obsessed with them. I think the triple is the most exciting play in baseball."

Aaron hit 116 of those, twice collecting 14 in a single season.

When he retired as a player after the 1976 season, he said, "You can only milk a cow so long but then you're left holding the pail."

Retirement brought Aaron relative peace and quiet, elusive goals during the media frenzy that accompanied the race with Ruth.

"When the Babe Ruth thing was going on, I came to the park at two in the afternoon to sleep for a couple of hours," he said in 1973. "That was the only place it was quiet.

"Babe Ruth never had to contend with anything like that. I can't recall a day this year or last when I did not hear the name of Babe Ruth."

Just as times change in baseball, so do economic conditions.

"Some of the players these days," a frustrated Aaron said during his days as Atlanta's player personnel director, "walk in with a suitcase full of money and a cell phone against their heads. I can't tell them anything."

He had better luck with three-dozen teenagers from the Cuban national team when he invited them to his home for a barbecue before the 1996 Summer Olympics in Atlanta.

"They'll be strangers when they come over here," he said, "but I wanted to make them feel at home." Spanish-speaking daughter Ceci was the official translator for the event, which followed a trip to Cuba that provided a platform for Aaron to meet Fidel Castro.

After posing with Ted Turner, wife Jane Fonda, and the bearded Cuban leader, Aaron said, "All I know is I talked to Castro and they treated me very well."

Official Baseball came around much more slowly.

"I broke one of the most prestigious records," Aaron said in 1999, "but was baseball ready to accept it? I don't think America was ready to accept it."

Nor was the country ready to accept the idea of a Black manager, general manager, or executive whose recommendations would receive serious consideration. Aaron and former brother-in-law Bill Lucas, both hired by Ted Turner, finally broke the ice nearly thirty years after Jackie Robinson integrated the game.

Aaron once ended a Turner Broadcasting board meeting with a strong criticism of the Braves. "This team is so slow it will take four singles to score a run," he said.

Breaking Babe Ruth's record empowered Aaron, once considered shy and introverted by teammates and media members.

"It's a great thing to be the man who hit the most home runs but it's a greater thing to be the man who did the most with the home runs he hit," Aaron explained. "As long as there's a chance that maybe I can hammer out a little justice now and then or a little opportunity here and there, I intend to do as I always have—keep swinging.

"Once the record was mine, I had to use it like a Louisville Slugger. I believed there was a reason why I was chosen to break the record. I felt it was my task to carry on where Jackie Robinson left off and I knew only one way to go about it. It was the only way I ever had of dealing with things like fastballs and bigotry."

From Bob Costas

"It was about staring down some of the worst of America and prevailing as an enduring symbol about what can be best about America."

—Broadcaster Bob Costas on Aaron's record

Deceptive Looks

"Baseball is a lot like the ivy-covered wall of Wrigley Field—it gives off a great appearance but when you run into it, you discover the bricks underneath. At times, it seems like we're dealing with a group of men who aren't much different than others we've all run into over the years, except they wear neckties instead of robes and hoods."

—Hank Aaron

Making a Difference

"Baseball needs me because it needs somebody to stir the pot and I need it because it's my life. It's the means I have to make a little difference in the world."

—Hank Aaron

Veggie Heaven

"I was a vegetarian before people knew what a vegetarian was. My father didn't make much money so all I ate was vegetables."

—Hank Aaron on growing up poor in Mobile

Andrew Young's Tribute

"Just his presence before he ever got a hit changed this city."

—Former Atlanta Mayor Andrew Young

Hank on Hitting

"Getting base-hits was the greatest thrill of my life. I was strictly a guess hitter, which meant I had to have a thorough knowledge of every pitcher I came up against and develop a strategy for hitting him. My method was to identify the pitches a certain pitcher had and eliminate all but one or two and then wait for them. One advantage I had was quick wrists. Another advantage—and one that all hitters have—was my eyesight. Sometimes I could read the pitcher's grip on the ball before he ever released it and be able to tell what pitch he was throwing."

—Hank Aaron's hitting philosophy

Brother Trouble

Jack Billingham, who threw the gopher ball that allowed Hank Aaron to tie Babe Ruth, surrendered home runs to both Aaron brothers.

Longevity Counts

Asked in 1974 if he considered himself lucky to have spent his entire career with the Braves, Hank Aaron had a quick response: "No, *they're* lucky," he said.

Koufax vs Aaron

"When Hank walked up to the plate, he was so relaxed he looked as if he were sleeping. He looked that way until he swung the bat."

—Sandy Koufax

186

Sandy and Hank

"Now that we are both Hall of Famers, I get to see [Henry] in those types of situations as opposed to facing him in the batter's box. I prefer that meeting much better."

—Sandy Koufax

Fergie's Take

"Just when you've thrown the ball by him, he's got the bat around so fast that he almost takes the ball out of the catcher's glove."

—Ferguson Jenkins

Seaver's Idol

"When I was a youngster," Hall of Famer Tom Seaver once said, "Henry Aaron was the supreme type of ballplayer I wanted to be. He was a dedicated man with super ability. My impressions of him never changed."

G.O.A.T.

"Hank Aaron is without a doubt the greatest righthanded hitter I've ever seen—ahead of Joe DiMaggio."

—Donald Davidson in *Caught Short*

Fence Busters

A few years after Hank Aaron and Eddie Mathews appeared together on a Topps card called "Fence Busters," he suggested moving the outfield fences in during his four-year stint on the board of the Atlanta Stadium Authority. "The one recommendation I made was to bring the fences in five feet," he said. "Now that I'm not on the Authority, they're moving the fence back five feet but only in right field. I hadn't hit a ball to right field in six years. They're leaving the left-field fence alone."

Smart Answer
When a reporter asked him what he looked for at the plate, Hank Aaron said, "The baseball."

Sleepy Curves
Breaking Babe Ruth's record was such an obsession for Hank Aaron that he dreamed about it. "How can I forget it?" he said. "I'd like to play until I can't anymore. Then I'll take a full year off and get to think like the average man. I won't have to jump out of the way of curve balls in my sleep."

Song & Dance Man?
After he signed with WMA Sports, a subsidiary of the William Morris Agency, Aaron announced he would do commercials and endorsements—without singing or dancing. "I can't sing and I can't dance," he told a media conference called to make the announcement, "so there's no use making a fool out of myself. I don't think that's what we're talking about. At least I *hope* not."

Together Forever
"I was Henry's teammate and played alongside him longer than any other player. Longer than Eddie Mathews or Warren Spahn or any of those guys. When he used to come to the ballpark, I watched how he put on his uniform, how he went out and took batting practice, and how he took infield practice. Henry was never flashy, he never did any showboating, and he never sought

the spotlight. Henry Aaron just went out and played the game the way it should be played."

—Phil Niekro

Nolan's Memories

"I used to follow his career when I was a teenager and he played for the Milwaukee Braves. In fact, I had to face Henry Aaron in one of my very first games ever when I made it to the big leagues. I was just 19 years old and was with the New York Mets and the game was in Shea Stadium. I was called in from the bullpen to face Henry and a Braves team that also included Joe Torre, Eddie Mathews, and all those great players. I guess you can say I was thrown into the proverbial fire very early."

—Nolan Ryan

CHAPTER 16
ODDITIES & IRONIES

The longer a star lasts, the longer the list of oddities and ironies that most casual fans might not realize. Hank Aaron was no exception.

For example:

- In his first appearance for the Indianapolis Clowns of the Negro American League in 1952, Hank Aaron turned five double plays and went 10-for-11 in a double-header.
- Former Boston Braves manager Tommy Holmes thought Hank Aaron would not make the majors. "He'll never play Major League Baseball," said Holmes, runner-up for the 1945 MVP award after finishing second in the NL with a .345 average. "He can't pull the ball."
- When Aaron's average fell to .279 in 1966, the culprit was an injured left leg that pained him much of the season.
- Although he finished with a fine .305 lifetime average, Aaron believed he could have added 10 to 20 points to that mark had he become a switch-hitter.

- Braves who wore No. 44 before Hank Aaron: Bob Chipman (1951) and Buzz Clarkson (1952) in Boston.
- Brewers who wore No. 44 before Hank Aaron: Hank Allen (1970) and Gorman Thomas (1973–1974).
- Aaron was the first Milwaukee Braves player to wear No. 44 and the first Atlanta Braves player to wear No. 44.
- No. 44 has been retired both by the Braves and the Brewers.
- Hank Aaron stole 30 bases in a season only once, during his 30/30 year in 1963.
- He was the third 30/30 man in baseball history, after Willie Mays and Ken Williams.
- Atlanta Mayor Maynard Jackson led an unsuccessful campaign to have Fulton County Stadium renamed Hank Aaron Stadium.
- Statues of Hank Aaron stand outside three different ballparks.
- He received medals from two different presidents.
- His picture appeared on a box of Wheaties, billed as the "breakfast of champions."
- Astrologist Jeanne Dixon predicted Hank Aaron would not break Babe Ruth's record—prompting Braves publicist Lee Walburn to quip, "Yeah, but she doesn't have to pitch against him."
- After Aaron hit a ball over the roof in left field at Connie Mack Stadium, bullpen catcher Gene Oliver went outside to measure it, determining it was over 600 feet to where the ball had rolled under a car in the parking lot.
- Aaron hurt his knee in a 1970 collision with Giants catcher Dick Dietz and needed more rest as a result.

- When Muhammad Ali fought Joe Frazier for the first time, on March 8, 1971, Aaron was among the star baseball players who left spring training camps to see it via closed circuit in a Fort Lauderdale theater, along with future Hall of Famers Mickey Mantle, Frank Robinson, Brooks Robinson, Whitey Ford, and Phil Rizzuto.

- On May 8, 1971, Willie Mays hit his 634th home run and Hank Aaron hit his 604th, marking the first time two members of the 600 Home Run Club connected in the same game, a 5–2 Braves win over the Giants in Candlestick Park.

- Aaron's .669 slugging percentage in 1971 was the best by a National League batter since Stan Musial's .702 in 1948.

- A versatile player, Aaron played 71 games at first base and 60 in the outfield in 1971.

- Hank Aaron and Dale Murphy used identical bats, weighing 33 ounces and measuring 35 inches long, as opposed to Babe Ruth's 40-ounce, 36-inch model.

- Aaron thrilled 35,000 admirers at "Hank Aaron Night" in Milwaukee County Stadium in 1973 with a home run against Billy Parsons during an exhibition game between the Braves and Brewers. "He had been gone from the constant view of the Milwaukee fans for seven years," said Brewers infielder Don Money, "but obviously had not been forgotten. Many of the people in the stands had tears running down their faces as Aaron rounded the bases."

- With Ruth's record so close he could almost taste it, Aaron hit .398 between the 1973 All-Star Game on July 24 and the end of the season.

- Babe Ruth's record stood for thirty-nine years; Hank Aaron's stood for thirty-three.
- The pitcher who caught Aaron's 715th in the Braves bullpen, an obscure left-handed reliever named Tom House, went on to enjoy the best year of his eight-year career (6–2, 1.93 ERA) in the months that followed.
- Aaron threw out the first pitch at the 2000 All-Star Game in Atlanta.
- When Aaron was inducted into the National Baseball Hall of Fame, one of the other four inductees was Happy Chandler, commissioner of baseball in 1947, when he overruled club owners and allowed the Brooklyn Dodgers to sign Jackie Robinson.
- The final game of the Boston Braves—with Aaron still in the minors—drew 4,694 fans.
- On March 14, 1954, Aaron was a twenty-year-old rookie who had three hits, including a home run, in his first exhibition game.
- He led the majors in OPS (on-base plus slugging) in three different decades.
- Aaron finished first in total bases eight times and extra-base hits five times.
- He hit three of his 755 home runs as a pinch-hitter, seven as a second baseman, and a record 124 in the first inning.
- After turning thirty-five, he hit 245 home runs with at least 34 home runs each year.
- A great contact hitter, he averaged 63 strikeouts a year.
- Exactly 400 of his home runs came with the bases empty.
- Aaron hit .300 in 14 different seasons.

- The uniform No. 5 Aaron wore as a rookie in 1954 was later worn with distinction by two other sluggers: Bob Horner (four home runs in a game in 1986) and Freddie Freeman (National League MVP in 2021).
- Aaron became the first man to have his number retired by two different teams.
- In the 1959 postseason, Hank Aaron won more rounds of *Home Run Derby*, a syndicated TV show, than anyone else, taking home $30,000—nearly two years of his salary at the time.
- Over a career that stretched twenty-three years, he averaged 37 home runs per 162 games.
- He hit .362 with six home runs and 16 RBIs in 17 postseason games over three years.
- In world baseball history, Henry ranks third with 755 home runs, trailing Nippon Professional League slugger Sadaharu Oh (868) and Barry Bonds (763).
- Hank Aaron traveled 12 miles farther around the bases on his hits than any other batter in baseball history.
- Aaron played himself in an episode of ABC sitcom *Happy Days* and also in an episode of *Futurama* called "A Leela of Her Own."
- Aaron and Eddie Mathews homered in the same game 75 times, a record for teammates.
- A versatile player, Aaron played 2,174 games in right field, 308 in center, 315 in left, 210 at first base, 43 games at second, and seven games at third.
- Aaron and Babe Ruth were both paid better than the presidents who saw them play.

- After making personal appearances on the campaign trail for John F. Kennedy in 1960, Jimmy Carter in 1976, and Bill Clinton in 1996, Aaron was credited by all three for helping them become President of the United States.
- Bobby Bonds, father of Barry, was in right field for the Angels on July 20, 1976, when Aaron hit his 755th and last home run.
- Aaron led the National League in home runs four times and matched his uniform number with four 44-homer seasons, including one in which he tied another 44, Willie McCovey.
- Hank Aaron was the victim when Sandy Koufax recorded his first strikeout.
- Aaron hit the last home run by a Milwaukee Braves player at Milwaukee County Stadium.
- The Mobile BayBears, a Double-A team, play in Hank Aaron Stadium. No major-league park has ever been named after a player.
- A schoolboy football star in Mobile, Henry later became a huge fan of the Cleveland Browns—even spending time at their training camp in Mentor, Ohio and subscribing to *Browns News*, the team's newsletter.
- Daughter Dorinda was born on Hank's birthday, February 5, in 1962.
- Henry homered in an exhibition game on "Welcome Home Henry Night" in Milwaukee, on May 6, 1974.
- Hank Aaron hit his first grand-slam in 1957, his fourth season.

- When Japanese home run king Sadaharu Oh hit his 715th home run on October 11, 1976, the on-deck hitter was Davey Johnson, the same man who was in the hole when Aaron hit his 715th. The only other man to be a teammate of both home run kings was Jack Lind, who played for the Milwaukee Brewers during Aaron's two-year tenure (1975–1976) with the then-American League club.

- Aaron beat Oh, 10–9, in a home run hitting contest in Japan on November 2, 1974, but Oh became the world home run king when he hit his 756th home run on September 3, 1977.

- Six men pinch-hit for Hank Aaron: Lee Maye, Mike Lum, Marty Perez, and Johnny Blanchard with the Braves and Johnny Briggs and Mike Hegan with the Brewers.

- Take away Aaron's 755 home runs and he still had 3,016 hits. He hit 2,294 singles.

- Aaron liked the color blue. Although red was traditionally the primary color used in Braves uniforms, the team changed to a blue-dominated motif in 1972 after Aaron said he was partial to that color. He was wearing the blue-and-white uniform when he broke Babe Ruth's record in 1974.

- Often overlooked because he played the same position (right field) as Roberto Clemente, Aaron won consecutive Gold Gloves from 1958 to 1960.

- Aaron started and finished his career as a left fielder. He spent his first (1954) and last (1974) Atlanta years there. During his final two seasons, Aaron was a designated hitter for the Milwaukee Brewers.

- Although Aaron's best home run season was 1971, when he hit 47, other sluggers who also failed to exceed that level in a single season included Ernie Banks, Johnny Bench, Joe DiMaggio, Rogers Hornsby, Reggie Jackson, Eddie Mathews, Willie McCovey, Stan Musial, Mel Ott, Duke Snider, Ted Williams, and Carl Yastrzemski.
- While Aaron played, only eight others topped 47 home runs in a season (on 13 different occasions).
- During his tenure in Milwaukee, Aaron hit more home runs on the road (213) than at County Stadium (185).
- Analytics expert Bill James said in the 1986 *Historical Baseball Abstract* that Aaron would have enjoyed several 50-homer seasons during his peak years had he been playing home games in an "average" home run park rather than Milwaukee County Stadium.
- Philadelphia pitcher Ray Culp gave up Hank Aaron's last home run as a Milwaukee Brave and first home run as an Atlanta Brave.
- One of Aaron's 755 home runs went almost unrecognized because it occurred on July 3, 1966—the same date *pitcher* Tony Cloninger hit two grand-slams and knocked in nine runs for the Braves against the Giants.
- Atlanta Fulton County Stadium was certainly "the Launching Pad" for Aaron, who had four of his 40-homer seasons while playing there between the ages of thirty-two and forty.
- Although Babe Ruth hit at least 20 home runs on the road 13 times, Aaron ranks second (tied with Harmon Killebrew and Willie Mays) for second place with six.

- Aaron retired not only as the all-time home run king (755) but as the king of road home runs (370). Both records are now held by Barry Bonds (762 and 383, respectively).
- Aaron, Ruth, and Bonds were the only men who averaged 35 home runs a season for two decades.
- Hank Aaron matched or topped his uniform number 44 three times in Milwaukee because of his ability to hit home runs on the road.
- At 1,050 feet above sea level, Atlanta Fulton County Stadium was an especially friendly target in 1971, when an aging Aaron hit 31 home runs at home and 16 on the road.
- The Aarons (768) hit more home runs than any brother tandem, including the DiMaggios (573), Boyers (444), and Alous (269).
- Aaron, Willie Mays, and Barry Larkin were the first three Hall of Famers who hit 30 home runs and stole 30 bases in the same season.
- A Triple Crown threat who never won one, Aaron took two batting titles to accompany his four home run titles and four RBI championships but never won all three Triple Crown legs in the same year.
- Aaron never hit for the cycle: a single, double, triple, and home run in a game.
- One-time Aaron teammate Lee Maye sang with The Platters before they started making records.
- A barnstorming team organized by Willie Mays after the 1955 season featured six future Hall of Famers: Ernie Banks, Roy Campanella, Larry Doby, Monte Irvin, Mays, and Aaron.

- Because Bradenton was still segregated during 1957 spring training, Aaron and other Blacks on the Braves stayed in the home of schoolteacher Lulu Gibson.
- Only 1,362 fans, the smallest crowd in Atlanta history, turned out to witness Aaron's 711th career home run on Sept. 17, 1973, against San Diego.
- Hank Aaron hit 10 home runs while Carl Morton was pitching for the Braves in 1973.
- He singled in his last at-bat for hit No. 3,771, third only to Pete Rose and Ty Cobb.
- He tied Ruth with 2,174 runs scored, trailing Cobb by 71.
- When Hank Aaron retired in 1976, only eight players plus Ruth had ever hit 50 home runs in a season.
- As director of player development for the Braves, Hank Aaron recommended that brother Tommie be promoted to manager of AAA Richmond, where he did a good job.

CHAPTER 17
AFTERMATH

————————————

June 18, 1974, was "Henry Aaron Day" in New York. Not in Milwaukee or Atlanta, but New York.

The same city that he had tormented in the 1957 World Series against the Yankees and the 1969 National League Championship Series against the Mets was now paying him the ultimate tribute.

Mets fans despised the Braves, who made a habit of winning strings of National League East titles and limiting the Mets to wild card contenders or worse, but they loved heroes. And Hank Aaron was a hero, especially in his waning years.

"Henry Aaron Day" helped make up for all those years he was overlooked everywhere but his home in the Deep South.

Arranged by official proclamation of Mayor Abe Beame and Governor Malcolm Wilson, festivities for the forty-year-old superstar included a motorcade through Harlem and a City Hall ceremony in which he was given the keys to the city.

Even Bowie Kuhn, the commissioner conspicuous by his absence two months earlier when Aaron broke Babe Ruth's record, showed up at Shea Stadium the night before for a handshake and home-plate ceremony.

At the ballpark, the Mets presented Aaron with a commemorative plaque, along with a rocking chair.

In thanking the team, he said, "I'm not quite ready for this yet. But I feel fine and I appreciate all the attention. I can't throw or run as good anymore but on any given day, I've still got as much bat-speed as ever and I can see the ball as well.

"Certain clubs still think they can throw the ball past you when you reach a certain age and that's all right with me. But I'd rather retire a year too soon than a year too late when I'm stumbling around."

Aaron reiterated he was planning to retire after the season but was hoping to remain in the game.

"I wouldn't mind running a baseball club as general manager. I don't want to be a house boy, though—we've got enough of those. I want to make decisions."

Aaron, who also made a quick jaunt to Washington for a planned tribute from the House of Representatives, capped the day by accepting a Gold Medal, the city's highest award, as hundreds of government and sports officials, accompanied by civilian spectators, watched. Two of them were the widows of Babe Ruth and Lou Gehrig.

Under a banner that read "NEW YORK WELCOMES HANK AARON," the slugger told the crowd it was an honor to be saluted in the same town where Jackie Robinson opened the door for Blacks less than thirty years earlier.

"I was just fourteen years old when I heard Jackie speak in Mobile, Alabama and that inspired me," he told an estimated 5,000 schoolchildren at Mount Morris Park in Harlem. "Regardless of what anybody says, stay in school and get an education. If you try hard enough and just keep trying, you will reach the top."

Aaron had to bend over to receive the medal from the diminutive mayor, who stood only 5-foot-2 inches tall. It must have reminded him of being around Donald Davidson with the Braves.

"It is truly fitting that Hank Aaron receive this tribute from our city," Beame said. "A home run record has belonged to New York, thanks to Babe Ruth, for forty years. Now that Hank has the record, I think it is only fair that we have Hank too."

A mere shadow of his former self, Aaron finished the 1974 season with 20 home runs—half his previous year's total—and a .268 batting average in 112 games. His career mark stood at a solid .310 but he still thirsted for more, like a gambler who spins three sevens on a slot machine but can't walk away.

Rebuffed in a bid to manage the team after old friend Eddie Mathews was dismissed, Aaron was not offered an executive position either. Or at least not one that gave him any authority to make personnel decisions that influenced the team.

Clyde King, a former Dodgers relief pitcher from North Carolina, guided Atlanta to a surprising third-place finish with 88 wins, but Aaron had nothing left to prove there.

He homered in his last at-bat for the Atlanta Braves, against Cincinnati's Rawly Eastwick on October 2, 1974, to conclude his National League career with 733.

He was intrigued with the new designated hitter, implemented by the American League in 1973, and thought it could extend his career—especially if he could finagle his way back to Milwaukee. He still loved the city where he launched his major-league career in 1954 and had a strong friendship with Brewers owner Allan H. "Bud" Selig, who became commissioner of baseball in 1998. They even attended football games together before

Selig bought the Seattle Pilots and brought them to Milwaukee as the Brewers in 1970.

Aaron asked the Braves for a trade and a deal was arranged; the Brewers got the aging Aaron while the Braves obtained Dave May and Roger Alexander. Milwaukee wasn't much of a team then, but it did have Del Crandall, Aaron's old Milwaukee team-mate, as manager.

The Brewers also bestowed Aaron with a two-year contract calling for $240,000—not bad change in the years just before free agency broke baseball's financial bank wide open.

"It's a tremendous challenge," Aaron said of the move across league lines. "I'm sure a lot of things are involved other than playing. I'm not even sure I can play next year—with new pitchers, new towns, a whole new ball game for me. But I'm going to do the best I can."

Aaron also said he would not have accepted a move to any other city. "I'm happy to be back here for a lot of reasons," he said of his return to Milwaukee. "In the first place, I'd like to get one thing straight. When the thing first started about me coming to the American League, I didn't want any other clubs bidding for my services. I made up my mind Milwaukee would be the place I'd play. I would have quit baseball if I hadn't come to Milwaukee.

"It's a thrill not only playing baseball in Milwaukee but being back in a city which has been like home to me."

To make the Aarons feel at home, both signed with local media outlets—Henry on radio and Billye on television. "I can live anywhere," Hank told Lou Chapman of the *Milwaukee Journal*. "It's just the way the people are so friendly. It's not a case of just one person helping me; they've all been great.

"I've had a lot of thrills—the 715th home run and a lot that went before that—but I've got to consider my coming back here this year right up there."

Seeing all the WELCOME BACK, HENRY signs around town warmed his heart in the chill of the Wisconsin spring.

In the first American League game of his career, Aaron was greeted by nearly 48,000 fans who ignored brisk April weather to cheer their returning hero to the tune of "Hello, Dolly," subbing the name Henry in the title.

He was wearing the yellow-and-blue uniform of the Brewers when he became baseball's all-time RBI king on May 1, 1975, and extended his home run record to 755 when he connected against Dick Drago of the California Angels at Milwaukee County Stadium on July 20, 1976.

His last game came on October 3, 1976, but only 6,858 came to County Stadium to see it. The Brewers were 32 games out of first place and the Green Bay Packers football game, on television, provided strong competition. It was Aaron's 85th game, little more than half the season, and he was struggling, battling nagging injuries and unfamiliar pitches in strange new ballparks.

"I lost my desire to compete," admitted Aaron, who scratched out an infield single in his last at-bat. "I could feel it at the start of this season. The routine, the travel finally got to me."

Henry hit 22 home runs in two years for the Brewers, finishing his playing career in the same city where it began. But he knew his future sports activities would be restricted to golf, tennis, and racquetball, where his frequent partner was future Braves chairman Terry McGuirk.

Also a fan of spectator sports, he watched Tiger Woods make his pro golf debut in the 1996 Greater Milwaukee

Open. He later called Woods the most dominating athlete of all time.

As a member of the Atlanta Hawks board of directors, he convinced Ted Turner to complete a trade for basketball superstar Dominique Wilkins. He was on the board of the Atlanta Falcons as well, despite his passion for the Baltimore Ravens (nee Cleveland Browns).

Henry and Billye went to New York for the US Open tennis tournament, where they met the Williams sisters, Serena and Venus, and their father, Richard, who was also their coach. Aaron also had a tennis court added to his property. The house in southwest Atlanta also had a five-acre fish pond stocked with large-mouth bass that reminded Aaron of his many fishing expeditions on Mobile Bay.

The Aarons had a second home on a golf course in West Palm Beach, longtime Florida spring training home of the Braves.

"I was fooling myself that I was a golfer," he told writer Terence Moore, "but I got to be pretty good in tennis. I used to have all of the guys over to the house every Sunday after church to play tennis and we would get into little matches. You had everybody thinking they were better than what they were, including me, but I love tennis."

He also loved staying in shape, employing a trainer he met by accident at a Shoney's near his BMW dealership. He and Mykell Vital worked together for fourteen years.

The minute he hung up his spikes after the 1976 season, Henry Louis Aaron finally received the job offer he coveted: director of player development for the Atlanta Braves.

Selig, who shared Aaron's passion for football and hosted him for dinner at his home after games, wanted to keep him in Milwaukee but new Atlanta owner Ted Turner, the television magnate, was persuasive.

Aaron's post-playing career lasted thirty-eight years and expanded far beyond baseball.

He served as vice president of player development for the Braves, then stepped up to senior vice president and special assistant to the team president. He became corporate vice president of community relations for TBS television network, served on its board, and took on the title of vice president of business development for The Airport Network.

He had an office at CNN, Turner's all-news network, but moved it to Turner Field after the new ballpark—first opened for the 1996 Atlanta Olympics—supplanted Atlanta-Fulton County Stadium one year later. Aaron explained the move, saying he was most comfortable in the ballpark.

Aaron even carried home plate from Fulton County Stadium into Turner Field to make the move official.

Inside that ballpark was an elaborate museum named for Ivan Allen, the mayor most instrumental in luring the team from Milwaukee. The Atlanta section included an Aaron locker complete with the bat and ball involved in Home Run No. 715—formerly locked away in a bank vault—plus the 1995 World Series trophy, the first such prize ever won by an Atlanta team.

There was a Milwaukee section too, with a 1954 Topps Hank Aaron rookie card, Hartland statues of Aaron and Eddie Mathews, 1963 jerseys from Mathews and Warren Spahn, and a 1957 World Series ring.

"I'm glad the bat and ball are on display here," Aaron said of the museum. "It's theirs. I hit it here in Atlanta. It belongs to the people of Atlanta and the Southeast."

A full-sized Pullman sleeper car, depicting train travel as the primary way teams moved around during Aaron's early years, was also squeezed into the museum. "I remember riding the train," Aaron said, "but I don't remember it being that big."

Aaron's influence was also obvious in the 755 Club, an upscale 500-seat restaurant featuring photographs of Braves greats. A sequence of five oversized Aaron photos, all in black-and-white, highlighted the display.

In 1982, Aaron made a quick trip to Cooperstown for his own induction into the National Baseball Hall of Fame, but even then was almost anonymous to the majority of baseball fans who had forgotten his race with Ruth's record.

Selig, seizing a long-overdue opportunity, then created the Hank Aaron Award, the first award named after a player who was still living and the first of any kind to be introduced in more than thirty years. Started in 1999 as a sixty-fifth birthday present to Aaron, the award has been given ever since to the top hitter in each league.

Future winners could even come from the Hank Aaron Rookie League program, which the slugger founded, or other new ventures designed to attract Blacks and other minorities into Major League Baseball. Selig asked Aaron to help develop those initiatives, with the support of MLB.

In 2002, Aaron received the Presidential Medal of Freedom, the nation's highest civilian honor. He met nine presidents—which may be another record—and campaigned for at least four of them, namely John F. Kennedy, Jimmy Carter, Bill Clinton, and Barack Obama. He never could figure out why Jackie Robinson, his personal hero and inspiration, was a Republican.

Carter became a close personal friend, not only hosting Aaron in the Oval Office but even skiing together in Colorado, part of a four-day annual Carter Foundation event for ten to twenty kids living in low-income areas. Both Aaron and Carter were in their sixties when they went skiing for the first time, agreeing that downhill skiing is a difficult endeavor—even for a former professional athlete.

A regular at Braves games in Atlanta, Carter was present the night Hank hit No. 715.

"As governor, I had our state make me an automobile tag that said HLA 715," he remembered, "but the Chamber of Commerce and people of Atlanta took up a collection and gave Hank a new Cadillac. I got ten times more publicity with that tag, since it was unique, than the Chamber did with its $12,000 Cadillac. Hank and I have joked about how I was a skinflint who gave him a $10 tag, which got all the publicity."

Like Carter, Clinton was a little-known moderate Southern governor seeking higher office when he sought Aaron's help. Clinton credited Aaron with helping him carry Georgia in 1992 because of an Atlanta rally Hank and US Senator Sam Nunn helped organize. No Democrat had won the state since Carter in 1976.

"We had a rally in a football stadium outside Atlanta in the weekend before the election and filled it," Clinton recalled. "Hank Aaron was there, and we had 25,000 people. Then we won the state by 13,000 votes. So everyone at that rally can fairly claim to have made me President of the United States."

"When I tell everyone that Hank Aaron is a big reason I became President of the United States," said Clinton, "it's not just hyperbole because I love the man. I say it because it's true."

Years later, before his second term finished, Clinton presented the home run king with the Presidential Citizens Medal for "exemplary service to the nation."

Never a figurehead in the Atlanta front office, Aaron worked with scouting chief Paul Snyder to find, sign, and develop such future stars as David Justice, Ron Gant, Tom Glavine, and Steve Avery. Aaron also had the difficult job of cutting his own son, Lary, and a minor-league catcher named Brian Snitker.

Aaron saw something in Snitker, who spent forty-six years in the organization as coach, scout, and minor-league pilot before winning six straight NL East division crowns and a world championship as manager of the Atlanta Braves.

"I went into DeKalb College to work out and I saw him walking around," Snitker revealed. "That was his first year back in Atlanta. I was in Double-A and threw a lot of batting practice. He called me one day and wanted me to go to Rookie League in Bradenton, Florida, and work with the club as pitching coach.

"Then he gave me a job as roving instructor and my first managing job—in Anderson, South Carolina. He gave me the ability to develop young players. He didn't micro-manage; he trusted you. Every one of us wanted to do a very good job for Hank. Just the fact that he trusted you to do that job was huge.

"He was always right there for me. Anytime I called, he answered the phone. Anything he could do for me, my family, he was always a big advocate of mine and pulled for me. Anytime anything good happened in my career, he would call to congratulate me."

As for son Lary, Father knew best. "I saw him going no higher than A ball," Aaron said of cutting his son. "I told him he had two choices: staying in A ball or going back to college, getting a degree, coming back out, and having a family."

Lary reluctantly agreed, went back to school, and eventually became a schoolteacher and long-time scout for the Milwaukee Brewers.

Ralph Garr, whose Atlanta career was starting when Aaron's was ending, also was hired by Henry. At the 1984 Baseball Winter Meetings in Houston, he landed a job as scout and minor-league base-running coach after expressing interest in rejoining the Braves, who had traded him away in 1975. Aaron was director of player development at the time.

"I enjoyed every minute of it," Garr said. "I was able to watch Tom Glavine, John Smoltz, Chipper Jones, Andruw Jones and all those wonderful ballplayers come up through the Braves organization. It all started because Hank Aaron called me. I went down to the winter meetings as a friend and ended up being hired."

After he retired, Aaron was a regular spring training presence, dashing off to the back fields in a golf cart to check in on young players who might amount to something with the proper coaching. Snitker often went with him.

Always outspoken about keeping steroids and other drugs out of the game he loved, Aaron taped a Super Bowl XLI commercial with Barry Bonds in which he kiddingly suggested that Bonds retire before breaking Aaron's record. When Bonds finally did it, on August 7, 2007, a taped congratulatory video from Aaron was shown on the San Francisco scoreboard. But he was not there in person.

Although he always insisted that records were made to be broken, he disdained the alleged steroids cheats with a ferocity that came to a head on May 7, 2015. Widely considered the elder statesman of the game at the age of eighty-one, he unleashed a tirade of criticism aimed squarely at those he felt inflated their records by using performance-enhancing substances.

"When you look at the whole situation and think about steroids," he said, "the game was made to be played right and if you can't play it right, you shouldn't play it at all."

Although he never realized his dream of becoming a manager or general manager, Aaron never turned his back on baseball. He even served on the Hall of Fame's Veterans Committee, which plays a part in who joins, after the death of incumbent member Pee Wee Reese in 1980.

Both inside and outside baseball, Hank Aaron was a diplomat and an ambassador. His painting was hung next to actor Morgan Freeman's in the National Portrait Gallery in Washington, DC, and he received the Order of the Rising Sun, Gold Rays with Rosette from Emperor Akihito of Japan.

Aaron's portrait was the fourth by Atlanta artist Ross Rossin to reach the gallery, along with Freeman, UN Ambassador Andrew Young, and poet Maya Angelou.

"You're on a different level when you get there," said Aaron, a spectator when Young's portrait was unveiled. "You've achieved a lot and somebody upstairs loves you. You feel like somebody special."

Rossin also painted Aaron's portrait for the Baseball Hall of Fame. "He is more than a sports star," the artist told the *Atlanta Journal Constitution*. "He is an unbelievable human being who represents the time he lived in."

Even though he never went to college, Aaron received numerous collegiate commendations. Tufts gave him an honorary Doctor of Public Service degree in 2000, Princeton presented an honorary Doctor of Humanities degree in 2011, and Tulane gave him a Doctor of Humane Letters degree—the first posthumous honorary degree ever given by the university.

The Vince Lombardi Cancer Foundation lauded him with the "Lombardi Award of Excellence" and the Georgia Historical Society, in conjunction with the state's governor, named him a Georgia Trustee in 2010. A stretch of trail along Milwaukee's Menomonee River was dubbed the "Hank Aaron State Trail" and a section of Capitol Avenue adjacent to Turner Field was named Hank Aaron Drive—giving the ballpark the street address of 755 Hank Aaron Drive. When the team later moved to suburban Cobb County, 10 miles away, the street number went with it.

Even after Jehovah's Witnesses took over the site of West Palm Beach Municipal Stadium, where the Braves held spring training for decades, the street leading to the entrance was named "Hank Aaron Way."

The section of left-field wall from Atlanta-Fulton County Stadium that stood under Home Run No. 715 survived the wrecking ball and is part of the new Georgia State ballpark built over the original site of Fulton County Stadium.

Although no big-league ballpark has been named for a player, there's a Hank Aaron Stadium in Mobile, Henry's boyhood home. And his actual boyhood home became a baseball museum. There's even a Hank Aaron Park in his hometown, which renamed Carver Park to honor him.

Aaron found time to throw out the first pitch at Truist Park, called Sun Trust Park when it opened in 2017, and at All-Star Games in both Milwaukee and Atlanta. He also attended his induction into the Wisconsin Athletic Hall of Fame in 1988.

Aaron was later ranked fifth by *The Sporting News* in its 1999 list of "100 Greatest Baseball Players."

The same scared kid who once looked like he was delivering a telegram to the spring training clubhouse of the Milwaukee Braves not only became a baseball hero—in the words of President Biden—but a community hero.

He and his wife Billye donated $4.2 million to the Atlanta-based Morehouse School of Medicine, which opened the Billye Suber Aaron Student Pavilion in 2017. The Aarons also gave more than $2 million in endowments and scholarships to Atlanta Technical College, which renamed its academic complex in Aaron's honor. On top of that, his Chasing the Dream Foundation funds 44 annual grants to the Boys & Girls Clubs of America.

Founded in 1999 at the All-Star Game in Boston, and with the full support of Selig and Major League Baseball, the Chasing the Dream Foundation was created to help 755 youngsters with educational and financial support. Ted Turner had already provided $100,000 in seed money and another $1 million, raised during a sixty-fifth birthday fund-raising soiree for Aaron, swelled the coffers.

Ten years later, Aaron received a special honor from the Baseball Hall of Fame when the "Chasing the Dream" exhibit opened in Cooperstown. Filled with photographs and career artifacts, it is one of only two permanent exhibits that honor a single player.

By that time, the Aarons had donated millions more, mostly to needy students wishing to pursue their education.

"Hank and Billye were literally the most giving couple I ever met," said Bob Hope, publicity director of the Atlanta franchise when it played like the Bad News Braves. "Their dedication to their scholarship program to give youngsters a chance to pursue their talents was very pure and honest."

Andrew Young, the former Atlanta mayor and UN Ambassador, agreed. "He probably gave more money away since his baseball days helping young people continue their dreams, develop their dreams than the money he made in baseball."

The last active player from the old Negro Leagues, he was an outspoken advocate for Black Americans—especially regarding opportunities in baseball. He also sat on the boards of foundations involved with everything from sickle cell anemia to cystic fibrosis, cancer, the Salvation Army, Easter Seals, the Boy Scouts, and Big Brothers/Big Sisters. The list also included the NAACP and an organization called PUSH (People United to Serve Humanity).

With corporate assistance from Arby's and Big Brothers/Big Sisters, the Hank Aaron Scholarship Program raised $5 million to send thousands of kids to college. He loved helping children in need whether they were Black or white.

"When most people think about me, they think about home runs," Aaron said, "but what I would like them to remember is that I was concerned about the well-being of other people."

He was thrilled to meet successful beneficiaries of his scholarships, and also made a point to hire needy minority kids for his restaurants. At one point, he owned seventeen of them, mostly in Georgia.

Somehow, he found the time to serve on the President's Council on Physical Fitness, represent the sports world on the list of ten best-dressed men in the country by the Customers Tailors Guild of America, and play in the American Airlines golf classic in Puerto Rico. He even showed up at Yankee Stadium for the 1986 season opener. It was a far cry from his previous experience there, as an outfielder for the Milwaukee Braves during the 1958 World Series.

He worked with Sadaharu Oh, the Babe Ruth of Japan, to develop baseball in Third World countries. He had first met Oh in Tokyo when the two home run champions staged their own Home Run Derby before 50,000 fans at Korakuen Stadium in Tokyo, on November 1, 1974. The event was apparently a big deal in Japan, as 2,000 reporters showed up at the airport to greet Aaron as he arrived. "Oh was much more of a national hero in Japan than I was in America," Aaron said after returning with his $50,000 prize from the winner-take-all competition.

Oh's slugging teammate Shigeo Nagashima was amazed by Aaron's performance. "I saw him play three times in spring training," he said of the celebrated American visitor. "He's a little fatter now but his batting hasn't changed. I'm very much surprised that he could step off an airplane and swing so well without any practice."

Aaron, forty at the time, won the contest over the thirty-four-year-old Oh by a score of 10–9. Both sluggers, using their own batting practice pitchers, aimed at fences that measured 300 feet down the lines and 390 feet to center in the horseshoe-shaped park. Each man was allowed to hit 20 balls—five in each of four "innings."

Six years later, with Aaron a little heavier and his bat a little slower, the home run king brought his Braves jersey out of mothballs again for a Home Run Derby in San Diego. After securing Warren Spahn as one of three pitchers, Padres promoter Andy Strasberg flew cross-country to invite Aaron personally. Under the Strasberg Rules, each batter would be allowed seven swings in each of his three at-bats.

In his first two trips to the plate, Aaron cleared the left-field fence four times, then stepped in against Spahn in a matchup that pitted the career home run champion against the pitcher with the most wins in the post-war era (and the most by any left-handed pitcher in baseball history). Spahn started with a brushback, then threw a screwball that broke down and away. A disappointed Aaron just dropped his bat and walked away, prematurely ending what had been a good-natured event. But the next day, he said of Spahn, "He's still a fierce competitor."

Aaron was a fierce competitor, too—as a player, baseball executive, and businessman. His nickname of "The Hammer," an abbreviated version of Hammerin' Hank, fit to a tee.

After Oh retired—with a world-record 868 home runs—he and Aaron decided over coffee to create an annual fair designed both to attract children to the game and to spread baseball's appeal worldwide. The result was the World Children's Baseball Fair, first held in Los Angeles in 1990. More than two-dozen have been held since.

Aaron loved cars almost as much as he loved home runs. Although he drove a Chevrolet Caprice for years, he later had three car dealerships, including one in Union City, Georgia, that offered autographed baseballs to anyone who purchased a BMW. Aaron, borrowing a page from the Bud Selig playbook, also owned dealerships that sold Honda, Hyundai, Land Rover, Mini, Scion, and Toyota until 2007, when he sold most of them.

Aaron also had multiple restaurant interests—from Arby's to Krispy Kreme and Church's, a competitor to Kentucky Fried Chicken—but also had a few failures, from real estate to too-good-to-be-true investments. As he did on the diamond, Henry dusted himself off and got right back in the box. A five-year, million-dollar deal with Magnavox also helped soften any previous losses.

Although he never made more than $240,000 a year play-ing baseball—nearly half-a-million less than the minimum sal-ary today—Aaron hit so many home runs off the field that he accumulated a net worth of some $25 million—twelve times his twenty-three-year total as a player, according to Terence Moore in *The Real Hank Aaron*.

Liked and respected for his honesty, humility, and sense of humor, he was honored for his integrity and experience. It just took way too long, according to his wife.

"It's amazing how his interests have changed," she said of Aaron, who once relaxed by watching soap operas and westerns. "I think he would have enjoyed business earlier, but the oppor-tunities didn't come."

Eventually, they did. Thanks in part to AFC Enterprises chair-man Frank Belatti, whose firm serves as parent company for Church's and Popeye's, Aaron developed the 755 Restaurant Corporation, with nearly two-dozen outlets in Georgia and the nearby Carolinas. He also promoted Lifebuoy Soap, Oh Henry! candy bars, and Coca-Cola, as much an Atlanta icon as Aaron himself.

"Hank wanted to be known for something besides hitting a baseball," Belatti told Jim Auchmutey of the *Atlanta Journal Constitution*. "He wanted to be respected as an entrepreneur."

Five—count 'em, five—Aaron statues stand at strategic locations for fans to see and remember. The one that gets the most traffic fifty years after the end of the Ruth race guards the entrance to Truist Park.

Hank Aaron baseball cards are a possession prized by millions of admirers. Topps alone produced more than seventy different versions over the years, including one where the negative was reversed. But an Aaron rookie in mint condition is a rare find and a valuable one: it sold for $357,594 during an auction in 2012.

A bottle of "Hammerin' Hank," a bold Cabernet Sauvignon created and produced by Baker Family Wines in California, isn't quite that costly. The Sacramento-area winery, owned by former Aaron protégé Dusty Baker, sold the wine for $60 a bottle after rolling out seventy cases in 2018. Baker began his backyard winery in 2005 and spends off-seasons working the vineyards.

He hooked Aaron as an investor after the home run king tasted Baker's product and asked whether he could produce a bold cab. Apparently, he could—using grapes raised in the nearby Sierra Foothills.

A man of great taste, Aaron attended many dinners, events, and tributes, but few so meaningful as the Hank Aaron Champion for Justice Awards sponsored by the National Center for Civil and Human Rights. "To be honest," he said that night in 2018, "I feel somewhat guilty I didn't possibly do as much as I could have done."

A once-gifted athlete, Aaron eventually encountered problems typical of getting older. He injured his hip when he slipped on a patch of ice outside his Atlanta home in 2014, which required a partial hip replacement, and needed the help of a cane and escort, usually wife Billye, to make subsequent public appearances. He also suffered from arthritis.

But Aaron rallied, made the arduous trip to Central New York, and received the loudest and longest standing ovation of anyone at the Baseball Hall of Fame Inductions in 2019 (incumbents share the dais).

He was just shy of his eighty-seventh birthday when he passed away on January 22, 2021.

Gone but not forgotten, Aaron has remained a larger-than-life Atlanta icon and American treasure.

Celebrities attended memorial tributes and fans placed flowers at his Truist Park statue and in front of the Fulton County Stadium wall that his 715th home run cleared.

Atlanta Mayor Keisha Lance Bottoms issued one of the most moving messages. "Derek, our family, and I join the nation in sending heartfelt condolences to Mrs. Billye Aaron, the beautiful wife of Henry 'Hank' Aaron for nearly fifty years, and the entire family. This is a considerable loss for the entire city of Atlanta. While the world knew him as 'Hammerin' Hank Aaron, because of his incredible, record-setting baseball career, he was a cornerstone of our village, graciously and freely joining Mrs. Aaron in giving their presence and resources toward making our city a better place. As an adopted son of Atlanta, Mr. Aaron was part of the fabric that helped place Atlanta on the world stage. Our gratitude, thoughts, and prayers are with the Aaron family."

A Truist Park memorial service, held on January 26, celebrated the life and legacy of the legend with the remarkable record. A musician appropriately named Henry—Henry Frantz—played the bagpipes in tribute.

The featured speaker was Braves manager Brian Snitker. Choking back emotion, he said, "I'm here today because of Hank Aaron."

No player spoke the next day at his three-hour funeral. But the president and dean of the Morehouse School of Medicine did.

"The world knows Hank Aaron as a trail-blazing athlete, a man who faced incredible odds as he beat Babe Ruth's home run record," said Dr. Valerie Montgomery Rice. "But to Morehouse School of Medicine, he was all that and much more. He was a stellar citizen, a businessperson, an advocate, a philanthropist, a mentor, and a friend."

After the service, Aaron was laid to rest at South-View Cemetery near the Rev. Martin Luther King Sr. A religious man, Aaron started and ended life as a Baptist, attending services at Friendship Baptist Church, but also spent many years as a Catholic.

The Braves honored him by painting the numerals 44 onto the outfield grass at Truist Park and included those numbers (and Phil Niekro's 35) on the back of team caps that season. When the team won the 2021 World Series, the voluminous championship ring, which physically opened, included 755 total diamonds and 44 emerald-cut diamonds. Before Hank Aaron, Jr. threw out the ceremonial first pitch of Game 3, the first World Series game in Atlanta that year, Dusty Baker bolted from the visiting dugout to greet Billye and other Aaron family members on the field.

The year-long Hank Aaron celebration had only one glitch but it was notable.

With the 2021 All-Star Game scheduled for Truist Park and an international television audience set to see it, the Braves had planned an elaborate memorial tribute. But they never got to stage it because Commissioner Rob Manfred—lobbied hard by Dodgers manager Dave Roberts—abruptly moved the game to Denver's Coors Field after objecting to the signing of allegedly restrictive voting laws by Georgia Governor Brian Kemp. The abbreviated Aaron tribute held there hardly had the same impact.

The impact of Aaron's loss reached far beyond baseball. The NFL's Atlanta Falcons, along with the Georgia Tech Yellow Jackets, temporarily retired the No. 44. So did the Gwinnett Stripers, the Triple-A affiliate of the Braves. And Forrest Hill Academy, named for a Confederate general who was also the Ku Klux Klan's first Grand Wizard, changed its name to Hank Aaron New Beginnings Academy.

In addition, the WSB broadcast containing Milo Hamilton's call of Henry's homer was selected for the National Recording Registry by the Library of Congress:

"There's a new home run champion of all time. And his name is Henry Aaron."

The Braves dedicated the 2021 season to Aaron, donating $1 million to the new Henry Louis Aaron Fund to bring Blacks into baseball and receiving another half-million from Major League Baseball and the Major League Baseball Players Association.

They asked fans to contribute $7.15 to the fund in April, the 47th anniversary of No. 715.

They created a Hank Aaron Weekend when the visiting team was the Milwaukee Brewers—by then playing in the National League Central Division—and handed out Aaron bobbleheads to fans who attended.

Truist Park already had Aaron tributes everywhere—film clips, videos, photographs, and a display of 755 bats representing each of his home runs. Although Aaron never actually played at Truist, he seemed to be a guiding force in the second-half surge that allowed the Braves to win the NL East title, the Division Series against the Milwaukee Brewers, the Championship Series against the Los Angeles Dodgers, and the World Series against the Houston Astros.

They did it despite the loss of Ronald Acuña Jr., who tore his ACL just before the All-Star Game, and a sluggish performance that left them with more losses than wins as August opened.

Every time the team donned its new City Connect uniforms, it created more Aaron memories.

"They were all about Hank—a great testament to the man," Snitker said. "We can't do enough in honor of Hank and what he meant to this organization and our team. We miss him dearly every year. It's nice that we're honoring his legacy and his memory the way we do."

Welcome Home Henry

Less than a month after he broke Babe Ruth's record in Atlanta, Hank Aaron returned to Milwaukee for "Welcome Home Henry Night." By the time he retired, he had hit 398 of his 755 major-league home runs for the Milwaukee Braves from 1954-65.

The Mystery Baseball

The ball Hank Aaron hit for his 755th and final home run, on July 20, 1976, was retrieved by Richard Arndt, a groundskeeper for the Brewers at Milwaukee County Stadium. Realizing its significance, he refused to surrender it and was not only fired but docked the $5 cost of the ball. Aaron unknowingly signed it at a Phoenix card show in 1994, but Arndt kept it five more years before selling it to wealth asset manager Andrew Knuth at auction for $652,000. Then a social worker, Arndt used his proceeds of $461,700 to help his children, his church, and Aaron's Chasing the Dream Foundation, which received $155,800.

A Korea Connection

Weeks after his 1982 induction to the National Baseball Hall of Fame, Hank Aaron was invited to tour South Korea, then enjoying its initial season of professional baseball. He watched games, held batting clinics, gave speeches, signed autographs, and met US and Korean military leaders who had followed his career. Invited to return that fall for a series of eight exhibition games between Korean teams and Braves minor-leaguers, Aaron accepted, coaching first base and participating in a home run derby with fellow Hall of Famer Ernie Banks, who played in the games at age fifty-one. Aaron said he hoped his trip would help defuse tension around the world through baseball.

EPILOGUE
THE GOLDEN ANNIVERSARY OF 715

Although Hank Aaron has been gone more than three years, his spirit still burns brightly.

That's because Major League Baseball, the Players Association, the Atlanta Braves, and especially Billye Aaron keep it alive.

She attends the annual Hank Aaron Awards presentations, visits Truist Park when time permits, and keeps in touch with such Braves alumni as Dusty Baker, who was in the on-deck circle when Hank broke Babe Ruth's record on April 8, 1974.

"It was one of the most exciting moments of our lives," she told Kelly Crull during a television interview last year. "It was such a fantastic evening. I was happy for him and for us.

"You don't get special moments that often. He came over to the box where I was sitting and we embraced. It was one of the most thrilling moments of my life aside from having married him."

Looking back, Billye said she could have jumped for joy. "When the moment passes, you don't know what to do or what to say other than praising the team and everyone who played a part. You end up jumping for joy."

As the calendar turned to 2024, the golden anniversary of the event fans once picked as the Most Memorable Moment in baseball history, her feelings have changed.

"I'm excited that he did it," she said just before Dr. Martin Luther King Jr. Day in January, "although it's very hard for me to celebrate anything now that Henry is gone. I try my best to uphold his legacy and understand what it would mean to him if he were here."

She admitted recognition was elusive for her late husband.

"Everybody seemed a little scared to jump into the ring because Babe Ruth held the record for so long," said the former TV talk show host and a tireless supporter of the United Negro College Fund. "It just didn't seem right to a lot of people that someone would come along and break that record—especially some Black kid.

"But we came to understand we live in a society that places less value on African-Americans than it does on other people. It was just something we had to come to grips with."

Snubs followed Aaron like Javert followed Jean Valjean.

"He was not happy with it," she said, referring to missed MVP awards and All-Star votes plus omissions from nine Hall of Fame voters. "I have to say in our situation, growing up where we grew up, both in the South, knowing how racism plays out, how people look at us and see us under a different magnifying glass, somehow if you keep your eye on the prize, you have to understand the situation under which you live."

Money was another issue. In 1976, his final season, Aaron earned $240,000—then tops in baseball, but now $500,000 less than the minimum salary a rookie earns in the major leagues.

"He regretted he wasn't in the money at the time but never resented the players," Billye said. "He said the players were getting what they deserved even though it was a lot more than he could have dreamed of at the time.

"He would just say on occasion, 'I think I could have gotten that salary.'

"He was an all-around good human being, a very decent human being, who often tried to help somebody along the way. He did a lot of that."

According to long-time family attorney Allan Tanenbaum, who spoke with his client regularly, Aaron was often asked what he thought of the multi-million-dollar salaries players make today. He would chuckle and say, "I'd go see Ted Turner and say, 'Hello, partner.'"

Turner bought the ballclub for $10 million in 1976 with an eye toward beefing up programming for his nascent TBS SuperStation. Aaron had already returned to Milwaukee but came back to Atlanta when the CNN founder offered him a coveted front-office job.

In the meantime, Aaron attempted to carry on the legacy left by Jackie Robinson, whom he first saw at age fourteen in his native Mobile, Alabama, when Robinson was on a speaking tour. The man who integrated baseball made an impression that lasted a lifetime.

Shortly after arriving in Atlanta, Aaron met with civil rights leaders Andrew Young, Martin Luther King Sr., and Martin Luther King Jr. He asked how he could become more involved in promoting the movement.

"We told him not to worry," Young said in an interview for the *Atlanta Journal Constitution*. "We told him to just keep hitting the ball. That was his job."

Dr. King was a big baseball fan and felt, along with the rest of the group, that Aaron's athletic prowess and status as the face of the game in the Deep South were sufficient—proving that the playing field finally was level. Young also compared Aaron to boxer Joe Louis, who beat white opponent Max Schmeling, and to Jackie Robinson, who braved bigotry to become an instant baseball star.

According to Billye, "Henry tried to show appreciation for all Jackie meant not just to African Americans but to Major League Baseball as a whole. He was very concerned about sharing that legacy and perpetuating that legacy with young people and especially young Black people who'd been denied that opportunity.

"I think he did a great job of keeping that legacy and trying to pass it on. He knew and understood what it meant to be poor and particularly to be poor in the south, where you were denied every opportunity. So we started the Hank Aaron Chasing the Dream Foundation to be able to assist young girls and boys to go after their dreams, to pull themselves out of bad situations and become full-fledged human beings who could help somebody else."

Asked about her husband's biggest achievement, Billye Aaron went beyond Ruth's record.

"The record was his way of making a name for himself in history," she said. "Otherwise they wouldn't have paid him any attention, I imagine.

"But his biggest achievement was as a human being. By the time he retired from baseball, his interests had grown. He was very interested in people. We had watched a documentary that grew his interest in trying to help little Black boys and girls become whatever they wanted to become but did not have the resources."

The Aarons met on her television talk show in 1973 just as the heat over the Race With Ruth was reaching red-hot readings.

"I sort of learned the game after I met Henry," she said. "It wasn't that I wasn't a big baseball fan—I just didn't know anything about it. I went to the game, sat down, and had Cracker Jack, peanuts, and Coca-Cola.

"To be honest, he didn't like watching the game with me because I asked too many questions and he wanted to focus on the game. It was how he reacted to baseball, how he appreciated baseball, and what it was doing to help us get ahead. I tried to learn as much as I could by osmosis and that's what I did."

She keeps in touch with numerous baseball contacts, especially Dusty Baker and former baseball commissioner Bud Selig, an Aaron friend from Milwaukee.

"Several of the players we were close to have also passed on," said Billye. "Frank Robinson, Joe Morgan, and Tom Seaver were good friends. I keep in touch with Dusty more than any of the others. In fact, Dusty just bought Henry's BMW a few weeks ago; he wanted it because it belonged to Henry."

If her busy schedule permits, Billye will visit Birmingham this summer to attend a game at Rickwood Field, the oldest surviving park used by the Negro Leagues and also the oldest to host professional baseball. She was invited to come to the stadium, built in 1910, by current commissioner Rob Manfred, like Selig a supporter of various initiatives in Aaron's name.

Shortly after Aaron died, the Braves created the Henry Louis Aaron Fund in conjunction with Major League Baseball and the Players Association. Initially endowed with $2.5 million, the money supports two Black Henry Louis Aaron fellows who work under Braves CEO Derek Schiller for one year, getting experience in the business side of baseball and building resumes they can present to interested teams and organizations.

Aaron was an outspoken advocate of bringing more African Americans into baseball—as players, managers, general managers, broadcasters, media members, or executives. Brother-in-law Bill Lucas had been the first de facto GM in the majors and Aaron himself hinted he might like to be a manager, general manager, or even Commissioner of Baseball.

"He might have been pulling somebody's leg," Billye said of those thoughts. "It may have entered his mind but I think it was wishful thinking. He knew it would never happen."

After he retired from the game, Aaron became a savvy and successful businessman, elder statesman, civil rights advocate, and revered and respected icon in the community and the country.

"Henry never glorified himself," said his widow, remembering that he got the loudest and longest standing ovation of any of the incumbent Hall of Famers at the 2019 Cooperstown inductions. "He never spent a lot of time trying to get glory or praise for what he'd done but was appreciative when it came. He was pretty quiet and withdrawn when it came to praising himself or when he got praise. At other times, we could bring up topics that often led to his saying, 'I'm glad it finally happened.' But he didn't make a lot of noise about it."

It was never about him but about how he could help other people, she noted.

Many people still consider him the home run king. But he hit even more home runs off the field.

Now a multi-faceted celebration will honor his life and legacy.

Though still in the discussion stages as this book went to press, the 50th anniversary of No. 715 will launch with pre-game ceremonies at Truist Park on Monday, April 8.

Many of the key players from April 8—from Dusty Baker and Darrell Evans to Davey Johnson and Ralph Garr—were expected to return to Atlanta to participate in pre-game ceremonies on the actual anniversary, along with Hall of Famer Joe Torre, who spent a huge chunk of his career as Aaron's teammate in Milwaukee and Atlanta.

In addition, the Baseball Hall of Fame's new "Souls of the Game" exhibit on Black baseball also includes Aaron, the last active major-leaguer whose career began in the Negro Leagues.

Statues in his honor are popping up everywhere, including the Louisville Slugger Museum in Kentucky and the Morehouse School of Medicine, which also has a Billye Aaron Pavilion saluting one of its benefactors.

"He had a number of accolades he never would have gotten had he not been the person he was," said Billye, who wears a pendant made from the 2021 Braves World Championship ring. "He was an outstanding human being who did what he could to help others. As he would put it, 'I just want to hammer out a little justice for some of these kids coming behind me.'"

Her only regret is not being able to celebrate the anniversary with the man who made it possible.

Asked whether she's excited about the year-long party, she said, "I am indeed. I just wish he could have been here for the 50th anniversary."

ATLANTA HISTORY CENTER TO UNVEIL HANK AARON EXHIBIT THIS APRIL

By Dan Schlossberg

(The following article appeared in *Forbes.com* on February 5, 2024.)

The day after the Atlanta Braves celebrate the 50th anniversary of Hank Aaron's 715th home run—which made him the lifetime leader—the Atlanta History Center will unveil an exhibit honoring the slugger's achievements both in and out of baseball.

Called *More Than Brave: The Life of Henry Aaron*, the exhibit will be on view to the public from April 9 through the 2025 All-Star Game at Atlanta's Truist Park.

Included will be artifacts, photographs, and memorabilia donated by the Braves, the Baseball Hall of Fame, the Aaron family, and multiple other sources.

Visitors will see the evolution of Aaron's baseball career, which began with a stint in the Negro Leagues but led to the Baseball Hall of Fame in Cooperstown. When he was inducted in 1982, he had more home runs, more extra-base hits, more runs batted in, and more total bases than any player in the history of the game.

"We hope this exhibition will serve as an inspiration to young people of all ages," said Billye Aaron, who was married to Henry from 1973 until his passing on Jan. 22, 2021. "This is an extremely proud moment for the Aaron family. We are more than delighted to join the Atlanta Braves and Atlanta History Center in celebrating the extraordinary life and legacy of our beloved Henry."

The Atlanta History Center announced the Aaron initiative on Feb. 5, which would have been Aaron's 90th birthday.

According to History Center president and CEO Sheffield Hale, "This collection not only honors his incredible talents on the baseball field but also his extraordinary strength of character that he demonstrated his entire career—but most poignantly during the quest for No. 715.

"Whether you are a devoted baseball fan, a lover of history, or simply curious about Aaron's remarkable life journey, we hope guests of all ages will leave inspired by his remarkable legacy."

Aaron played for the Milwaukee Braves from 1954-1965, went South with the team when it became the Atlanta Braves in 1966, and spent his final two seasons with the Milwaukee Brewers in 1975-76. He was a right-handed batter who played right field and made the All-Star team 25 times, a major-league record.

In addition to his on-the-field baseball exploits, the Aaron exhibit will depict his transition to successful front-office executive, also with the Braves, and businessman who found success as owner of restaurants and automobile dealerships.

He also became an outspoken advocate of civil rights after befriending fellow Atlanta residents Dr. Martin Luther King Jr., Andrew Young, and Ralph David Abernathy.

Thanks to the Atlanta Braves Foundation, the team honors Aaron's legacy through the Henry Louis Aaron Fund, established after his demise in 2021. The Fund supports his life-long passion to promote minority participation in baseball on the field and in the front office at all professional levels, including the minor leagues.

"Hank Aaron's 715th home run was one of the seminal moments in sports history and it will forever be etched in the memories of Atlantans and people around the globe," said Braves president and CEO Derek Schiller.

"The occasion of the 50th anniversary of that moment and this magnificent exhibit gives our organization and the broader Atlanta community an opportunity to celebrate this incredible man who inspired so many people. We also want to use this time to highlight the great work being done around the community in his name through the Henry Louis Aaron Fund."

Atlanta History Center, founded in 1926, is a 33-acre destination near the city's Buckhead section that includes the Atlanta History Museum, the Cyclorama, three historic homes, a research center, shop, café, and more. The Atlanta History Center Midtown includes the home of Margaret Mitchell, author of *Gone with the Wind*.

Atlanta History Center is open Tuesday-Sunday from 9-4. Further information may be found at AtlantaHistoryCenter.com.

Hank Aaron Hitting Stats (courtesy of Baseball-Refence.com)

Year	Age	Tm	G	AB	R	H	2B	3B	HR	GS	RBI	BB	IBB	SO	SH	SF	HBP	TB	BA	OBP	SLG	OPS
1954	20	Mil. Braves	122	468	58	131	27	6	13	0	69	28	0	39	6	4	3	209	.280	.322	.447	0.769
1955	21	Mil. Braves	153	602	105	189	37	9	27	0	106	49	5	61	7	4	3	325	.314	.366	.540	0.906
1956	22	Mil. Braves	153	609	106	200	34	14	26	0	92	37	6	54	5	7	2	340	.328	.365	.558	0.923
1957	23	Mil. Braves	151	615	118	198	27	6	44	1	132	57	15	58	0	3	0	369	.322	.378	.600	0.978
1958	24	Mil. Braves	153	601	109	196	34	4	30	2	95	59	16	49	0	3	1	328	.326	.386	.546	0.931
1959	25	Mil. Braves	154	629	116	223	46	7	39	0	123	51	17	54	0	9	4	400	.355	.401	.636	1.037
1960	26	Mil. Braves	153	590	102	172	20	11	40	0	126	60	13	63	0	12	2	334	.292	.352	.566	0.919
1961	27	Mil. Braves	155	603	115	197	39	10	34	1	120	56	20	64	1	9	2	358	.327	.381	.594	0.974
1962	28	Mil. Braves	156	592	127	191	28	6	45	3	128	66	14	73	0	6	3	366	.323	.390	.618	1.008
1963	29	Mil. Braves	161	631	121	201	29	4	44	2	130	78	18	94	0	5	0	370	.319	.391	.586	0.977
1964	30	Mil. Braves	145	570	103	187	30	2	24	0	95	62	9	46	0	2	0	293	.328	.393	.514	0.907
1965	31	Mil. Braves	150	570	109	181	40	1	32	0	89	60	10	81	0	8	1	319	.318	.379	.560	0.938
1966	32	Atl. Braves	158	603	117	168	23	1	44	1	127	76	15	96	0	8	1	325	.279	.356	.539	0.895
1967	33	Atl. Braves	155	600	113	184	37	3	39	1	109	63	19	97	0	6	0	344	.307	.369	.573	0.943
1968	34	Atl. Braves	160	606	84	174	33	4	29	1	86	64	23	62	0	5	1	302	.287	.354	.498	0.852
1969	35	Atl. Braves	147	547	100	164	30	3	44	1	97	87	19	47	0	3	2	332	.300	.396	.607	1.003
1970	36	Atl. Braves	150	516	103	154	26	1	38	1	118	74	15	63	0	6	2	296	.298	.385	.574	0.958
1971	37	Atl. Braves	139	495	95	162	22	3	47	0	118	71	21	58	0	5	2	331	.327	.410	.669	1.079
1972	38	Atl. Braves	129	449	75	119	10	0	34	1	77	92	15	55	0	2	1	231	.265	.390	.514	0.904
1973	39	Atl. Braves	120	392	84	118	12	1	40	0	96	68	13	51	0	4	1	252	.301	.402	.643	1.045
1974	40	Atl. Braves	112	340	47	91	16	0	20	2	69	39	6	29	1	2	0	167	.268	.341	.491	0.832
1975	41	Mil. Brewers	137	465	45	109	16	2	12	0	60	70	3	51	1	6	1	165	.234	.332	.355	0.687
1976	42	Mil. Brewers	85	271	22	62	8	0	10	0	35	35	1	38	0	2	0	100	.229	.315	.369	0.684
Career			G	AB	R	H	2B	3B	HR	GS	RBI	BB	IBB	SO	SH	SF	HBP	TB	BA	OBP	SLG	OPS
23 Years			3,298	12,364	2,174	3,771	624	98	755	16	2,297	1,402	293	1,383	21	121	32	6,856	.305	.374	.555	0.928

Hank Aaron Hits a Pennant-Winning Home Run!
Milwaukee Braves vs. St. Louis Cardinals
September 23, 1957

Box Score	1	2	3	4	5	6	7	8	9	10	11	R	H	E
St. Louis Cardinals	0	0	0	0	0	2	0	0	0	0	0	2	9	3
Atlanta Braves	0	1	0	0	0	0	1	0	0	0	2	4	14	0

Atlanta	AB	R	H	HR	RBI	BB	SO
Red Schoendienst 2B	6	1	2	0	0	0	0
Johnny Logan SS	5	1	1	0	0	0	1
Eddie Mathews 3B	6	0	1	0	1	0	0
Henry Aaron CF	4	2	3	1	2	2	0
Joe Adcock 1B	4	0	1	0	0	1	0
John DeMerit PR	0	0	0	0	0	0	0
Gene Conley P	0	0	0	0	0	0	0
Andy Pafko RF	5	0	1	0	0	0	0
Wes Covington LF	4	0	2	0	1	0	0
Del Crandall C	4	0	2	0	0	1	0
Lew Burdette P	4	0	1	0	0	0	1
Frank Torre PH-1B	1	0	0	0	0	0	0
	43	4	14	1	4	4	2

Atlanta	IP	H	R	ER	BB	K	HR
Lew Burdette	10	9	2	2	2	4	0
Gene Conley (W)	1	0	0	0	0	1	0
	11	9	2	2	2	5	0

St. Louis	AB	R	H	HR	RBI	BB	K
Don Blasingame 2B	5	0	0	0	0	0	0
Wally Moon CF	4	1	1	0	0	1	0
Stan Musial 1B	4	1	3	0	0	0	0
Dick Schofield PR	0	0	0	0	0	0	0
Joe Cunningham 1B	1	0	0	0	0	0	0
Irv Noren RF	4	0	1	0	0	1	1
Del Ennis LF	5	0	1	0	0	0	1
Al Dark SS	5	0	1	0	2	0	1
Hobie Landrith C	4	0	1	0	0	0	0
Ken Boyer PR	0	0	0	0	0	0	0
Hal Smith C	1	0	0	0	0	0	1
Eddie Kasko 3B	4	0	1	0	0	0	0
Vinegar Bend Mizell P	0	0	0	0	0	0	0
Larry Jackson P	3	0	0	0	0	0	1
Jim King PH	1	0	0	0	0	0	0
Billy Muffett P	0	0	0	0	0	0	0
	41	**2**	**9**	**0**	**2**	**2**	**5**

St. Louis	IP	H	R	ER	BB	K	HR
Vinegar Bend Mizell	1	4	1	1	0	0	0
Larry Jackson	7	7	1	1	2	1	0
Billy Muffett (L)	2.2	3	2	2	2	1	1
	10.2	**14**	**4**	**4**	**4**	**2**	**1**

Hank Aaron Hits 714!
Atlanta Braves @ Cincinnati Reds
April 4, 1974

Box Score	1	2	3	4	5	6	7	8	9	10	11	R	H	E
Atlanta Braves	3	0	0	1	2	0	0	0	0	0	0	6	6	0
Cincinnati Reds	1	0	0	0	1	0	0	3	1	0	1	7	13	1

Atlanta	AB	R	H	HR	RBI	BB	SO
Ralph Garr RF-LF	4	1	0	0	0	1	0
Mike Lum 1B-CF	5	2	3	0	0	0	1
Darrell Evans 3B	4	0	1	0	0	0	1
Henry Aaron LF	3	2	1	1	3	1	0
Rowland Office CF	0	0	0	0	0	0	0
Ivan Murrell PH	0	0	0	0	0	0	0
Frank Tepedino PH-1B	0	0	0	0	0	1	0
Dusty Baker CF-RF	5	1	1	0	0	0	0
Davey Johnson 2B	3	0	0	0	0	2	0
Johnny Oates C	4	0	0	0	0	0	1
Craig Robinson SS	5	0	0	0	0	0	1
Carl Morton P	3	0	0	0	0	0	2
Phil Niekro P	1	0	0	0	0	0	0
Tom House P	0	0	0	0	0	0	0
Jack Aker P	0	0	0	0	0	0	0
Norm Miller PH	1	0	0	0	0	0	1
Buzz Capra P	0	0	0	0	0	0	0
	38	6	6	1	3	5	6

Atlanta	IP	H	R	ER	BB	K	HR
Carl Morton	7	8	3	3	2	6	1
Phil Niekro	1.2	4	3	3	1	2	1
Tom House	0	0	0	0	1	0	0
Jack Aker	1.1	0	0	0	0	3	0
Buzz Capra (L)	0.2	1	1	1	1	1	0
	10.2	13	7	7	5	12	2

Cincinnati	AB	R	H	HR	RBI	BB	K
Pete Rose LF	5	3	3	0	1	1	0
Joe Morgan 2B	4	0	2	0	0	2	1
Dan Driessen 3B	4	1	2	0	0	0	1
Phil Gagliano PH	0	0	0	0	0	1	0
Tom Hall P	0	0	0	0	0	0	0
Clay Carroll P	0	0	0	0	0	0	0
Cesar Geronimo PH	0	0	0	0	0	0	0
Tony Perez 1B	5	1	2	1	4	0	1
Johnny Bench C	5	0	0	0	0	0	2
Ken Griffey RF	4	0	0	0	0	1	3
Merv Rettenmund CF	5	0	1	0	0	0	2
Dave Concepcion SS	5	1	2	1	1	0	1
Jack Billingham P	1	0	0	0	0	0	1
Andy Kosco PH	1	0	0	0	0	0	0
Roger Nelson P	0	0	0	0	0	0	0
Terry Crowley PH	1	0	0	0	0	0	0
Pedro Borbon P	0	0	0	0	0	0	0
George Foster PH	1	1	1	0	0	0	0
Darrel Chaney 3B	1	0	0	0	0	0	0
	42	7	13	2	6	5	12

Cincinnati	IP	H	R	ER	BB	K	HR
Jack Billingham	5	5	6	4	4	3	1
Roger Nelson	2	0	0	0	0	1	0
Pedro Borbon	2	0	0	0	0	1	0
Tom Hall	0.1	1	0	0	0	0	0
Clay Carroll (W)	1.2	0	0	0	1	1	0
	11	6	6	4	5	6	1

Hank Aaron Hits 715!
Atlanta Braves vs. Los Angeles Dodgers
April 8, 1974

Box Score	1	2	3	4	5	6	7	8	9	R	H	E	H	E
Los Angeles Dodgers	0	0	3	0	0	1	0	0	0	4	7	6	6	0
Atlanta Braves	0	1	0	4	0	2	0	0	X	7	4	0	13	1

Atlanta	AB	R	H	HR	RBI	BB	SO
Ralph Garr RF-LF	3	0	0	0	1	0	1
Mike Lum 1B	5	0	0	0	1	0	1
Darrell Evans 3B	4	1	0	0	0	0	0
Henry Aaron LF	3	2	1	1	2	1	0
Rowland Office CF	0	0	0	0	0	0	0
Dusty Baker CF-RF	2	1	1	0	0	2	1
Davey Johnson 2B	3	1	1	0	0	1	0
Leo Foster 2B	0	0	0	0	0	0	0
Vic Correll C	4	1	0	0	0	0	0
Craig Robinson SS	0	0	0	0	0	1	0
Frank Tepedino PH	0	0	0	0	1	1	0
Marty Perez SS	2	1	1	0	0	0	0
Ron Reed P	2	0	0	0	0	0	1
Johnny Oates PH	1	0	0	0	1	0	0
Buzz Capra P	0	0	0	0	0	1	0
	29	7	4	1	6	7	4

Atlanta	IP	H	R	ER	BB	K	HR
Ron Reed (W)	6	7	4	4	1	4	0
Buzz Capra (S)	3	0	0	0	1	6	0
	9	7	4	4	2	10	0

Los Angeles	AB	R	H	HR	RBI	BB	K
Davey Lopes 2B	2	1	0	0	0	1	1
Lee Lacy PH-2B	1	0	0	0	0	0	1
Bill Buckner LF	3	0	1	0	0	1	0
Jim Wynn CF	4	0	1	0	2	0	1
Joe Ferguson C	4	0	0	0	0	0	3
Willie Crawford RF	4	1	1	0	0	0	2
Ron Cey 3B	4	0	1	0	1	0	0
Steve Garvey 1B	4	1	1	0	0	0	1
Bill Russell SS	4	0	1	0	0	0	0
Al Downing P	1	1	1	0	1	0	0
Mike Marshall P	1	0	0	0	0	0	0
Von Joshua PH	1	0	0	0	0	0	1
Charlie Hough P	0	0	0	0	0	0	0
Manny Mota PH	1	0	0	0	0	0	0
	34	**4**	**7**	**0**	**4**	**2**	**10**

Los Angeles	IP	H	R	ER	BB	K	HR
Al Downing (L)	3	2	5	2	4	2	1
Mike Marshall	3	2	2	1	1	1	0
Charlie Hough	2	0	0	0	2	1	0
	8	**4**	**7**	**3**	**7**	**4**	**1**

Illustration by Ronnie Joyner

BIBLIOGRAPHY

Aaron, Henry with Furman Bisher, *Aaron: The Autobiography of the Greatest Home Run Hitter of the Modern Era*, New York: Thomas Y. Crowell Company, 1968.

Aaron, Hank with Dick Schaap, *Home Run: My Life in Pictures*, foreword by Ted Williams, Kingston, NY: Total Sports, 1999.

Aaron, Hank with Lonnie Wheeler, *I Had a Hammer: The Hank Aaron Story*, New York: HarperCollins, 1991.

Atlanta Journal Constitution staff, *Hank Aaron: A Tribute to the Hammer*, Chicago: Triumph Books, 2021.

Berkow, Ira, *Baseball's Best Ever: A Half Century of Covering Hall of Famers*, New York: Sports Publishing, 2022.

Berman, Len, *The 25 Greatest Baseball Players of All Time*, Napierville, IL: Sourcebooks, Inc., 2010.

Bisher, Furman, *Miracle in Atlanta: The Story of the Atlanta Braves from Boston to Milwaukee to Their Dazzling $18,000,000 Home in Atlanta*, Cleveland and New York: The World Publishing Company, 1966.

Broeg, Bob, *Super Stars of Baseball: Their Lives, Their Loves, Their Laughs, Their Laments*, South Bend, IN: Diamond Communications, 1994.

Bryant, Howard, *The Last Hero: A Life of Henry Aaron*, New York: Pantheon Books, 2010.

Buege, Bob, *The Milwaukee Braves: A Baseball Eulogy*, foreword by Eddie Mathews, Milwaukee: Douglas American Sports Publications, 1988.

Caruso, Gary, *The Braves Encyclopedia*, Philadelphia: Temple University, 1995.

Caruso, Gary, *Turner Field: Rarest of Diamonds*, Atlanta: Longstreet Press, foreword by Jimmy Carter, 1997.

Cohen, Robert W., *The 50 Greatest Players in Braves History*, Essex, CT: Lyons Press, 2023.

Cook, Kevin, *150 Years of Braves Baseball*, foreword by Hank Aaron, introduction by Terry McGuirk, Mendocino, CA: Skybox Press, 2020.

Davidson, Donald with Jesse Outlar, *Caught Short*, New York: Atheneum, 1972.

Dougherty, Steve and ESPN staff, *Hank Aaron: American Hero*, New York: Meredith Premier Publishing, 2021.

Couch, J. Hudson, *The Braves: First Fifteen Years in Atlanta*, Atlanta: The Other Alligator Creek Company, 1984.

Dewey, Donald and Acocella, Nicholas, Total *Ballclubs: The Ultimate Book of Baseball Teams*, Toronto: Sport Media Publishing, 2005.

Dickson, Paul, *Baseball's Greatest Quotations: An Illustrated Treasury of Baseball Quotations and Historical Lore*, New York: HarperCollins, 2008.

Eller, Buddy, Middleton, Gene, and O'Brien, Donald E., *The Amazing Braves: America's Team*, edited by May, Frank H., Atlanta: Philmay Enterprises, 1982.

Fields, Robert Ashley, *Take Me Out to the Crowd: Ted Turner and the Atlanta Braves, Huntsville*, AL: Strode Publishers, 1976.

Freedman, Lew, *Warren Spahn: A Biography of the Legendary Lefty*, New York: Sports Publishing, 2018.

Fuller, W. Jr., *Atlanta Braves: The First Twenty Years—A History*, Dallas: Taylor Publishing, 1986.

Hamilton, Milo and Schlossberg, Dan with Ibach, Bob, *Making Airwaves: 60+ Years at Milo's Microphone*, New York: Sports Publishing, 2007.

Honig, Donald and Ritter, Lawrence, *The Image of Their Greatness: An Illustrated History of Baseball from 1900 to the Present*, New York: Crown Publishers, 1979.

Hope, Bob, *We Could've Finished Last Without You: An Irreverent Look at the Atlanta Braves, the Losingest Team in Baseball for the Past 25 Years*, Atlanta: Longstreet Press, 1991.

Jacobson, Steve, *Carrying Jackie's Torch: The Players Who Integrated Baseball—and America*, Chicago: Lawrence Hill Books, 2007.

Joyner, Ronnie, *Hardball Legends and Journeymen: 333 Illustrated Baseball Biographies*, Jefferson, NC: McFarland & Company, 2012.

Kaplan, Jim, *The Greatest Game Ever Pitched: Juan Marichal, Warren Spahn, and the Pitching Duel of the Century*, foreword by Greg Spahn, Chicago: Triumph Books, 2011.

Klima, John, *Bushville Wins! The Wild Saga of the 1957 Milwaukee Braves and the Screwballs, Sluggers, and Beer Swiggers Who Canned the New York Yankees and Changed Baseball*, New York: Thomas Dunn Books, 2012.

Mathews, Eddie and Bob Buege, *Eddie Mathews and the National Pastime*, Milwaukee: Douglas American Sports Publications, 1994.

McCartney, Cory, *Tales from the Atlanta Braves Dugout: A Collection of the Greatest Braves Stories Ever Told*, New York: Sports Publishing, 2016.

McMane, Fred and Shea, Stuart, *The 3,000 Hit Club: Stories of Baseball's Greatest Hitters*, New York: Sports Publishing, 2012.

Money, Don with Herb Anastor, *The Man Who Made Milwaukee Famous: A Salute to Henry Aaron*, Milwaukee: Agape Publishers, 1976.

Moore, Terrence, *The Real Hank Aaron: An Intimate Look at the Life and Legacy of the Home Run King*, foreword by Dusty Baker, Chicago: Triumph Books, 2022.

Nathan, David H., editor, *The McFarland Baseball Quotations Dictionary, 3rd edition*, Jefferson, NC: McFarland & Co., 2011.

Neary, Kevin, *715: Reflections on Hammerin' Hank & the Home Run That Made History*, foreword by Monte Irvin, New York: Sports Publishing, 2015.

Nogowski, John, *Last Time Out: Big-League Farewells of Baseball's Greats*, Lanham, MD: Taylor Trade, 2005.

Onigman, Marc, *This Date in Braves History: The Complete History from Boston to Milwaukee to Atlanta*, foreword by Roy Blount, Jr., Briarcliff Manor, NY: Stein and Day, 1982.

Posnanski, Joe, *Why We Love Baseball: A History in 50 Moments*, New York: E.P. Dutton, 2023

Povletich, William, *Milwaukee Braves: Heroes and Heartbreak*, Madison, WI: Wisconsin Historical Society Press, 2009.

Prigge, Matthew J., *Opening Day in Milwaukee: The Brewers' Season Starters*, 1970-2022, Jefferson, NC: McFarland, 2023.

Purdy, Dennis, *The Team by Team Encyclopedia of Major League Baseball*, foreword by Tommy Lasorda, New York: Workman Publishing, 2006.

Reidenbaugh, Lowell, *100 Years of National League Baseball*, foreword by C.C. Johnson Spink, St. Louis: *The Sporting News*, 1976.

Rennert, Richard Scott, *Henry Aaron*, introductory essay by Coretta Scott King, New York: Chelsea House Publishers, New York and Philadelphia, 1993.

Ritter, Lawrence, and Honig, Donald, *The 100 Greatest Baseball Players Of All Time*, New York: Crown Publishers, 1981.

Rosengren, John, *Hammerin' Hank, George Almighty, and The Say Hey Kid: The Year that Changed Baseball Forever*, Napierville, IL: Sourcebooks, 2008.

Schlossberg, Dan, *Hammerin' Hank: The Henry Aaron Story*, New York: Stadia Sports Publishing, 1974.

Schlossberg, Dan, *The New Baseball Bible: Notes, Nuggets, Lists & Legends From Our National Pastime*, New York: Sports Publishing, 2020 edition.

Schlossberg, Dan, Pietrusza, David, Palmer, Pete, Gershman, Michael, and Thorn, John, *Total Braves*, Kingston, NY: Total Sports, 1996.

Stewart, Mark and Kennedy, Mike, *Hammering Hank: How the Media Made Henry Aaron*, Guilford, CT: Lyons Press, 2006.

Strasberg, Andy, *Home Runs: Tales of Tonks, Taters, Contests, and Derbies*, St. Louis Park, MN: August Publications, 2023.

Syken, Bill, editor, "Baseball's Greatest," New York: *Sports Illustrated*, 2013.

Thorn, John, *Baseball's 10 Greatest Games*, foreword by Tom Seaver, New York: Four Winds Press, 1981.

Tolan, Sandy, *Me and Hank*, New York: the Free Press, 2000.

Trutor, Clayton, *Loserville: How Professional Sports Remade Atlanta—and How Atlanta Remade Professional Sports*, Lincoln, NB: University of Nebraska Press, 2021.

Van Wieren, Pete and Klapisch, Bob, *The Braves: An Illustrated History of America's Team*, Atlanta: Turner Publishing, 1995.

Vascellaro, Charlie, Hank Aaron: A Biography, Westport, CT: Greenwood Press, 2005.

Vincent, David, *Home Run's Most Wanted: The Top 10 Book of Monumental Dingers*, Prodigious Swingers, and Everything Long-Ball, Washington: Potomac Books, 2009.

Wilbert, Warren N., *Baseball's Iconic 1-0 Games*, Plymouth, UK: Scarecrow Press, 2013.

INDEX